The Scandalous Affair of
MR KETTLE AND MRS MOON

A Comedy in Three Acts

by
J. B. PRIESTLEY

LONDON
SAMUEL FRENCH LIMITED

Copyright © 1956 by J.B. Priestley
All Rights Reserved

THE SCANDALOUS AFFAIR OF MR KETTLE AND MRS MOON is fully protected under the copyright laws of the British Commonwealth, including Canada, the United States of America, and all other countries of the Copyright Union. All rights, including professional and amateur stage productions, recitation, lecturing, public reading, motion picture, radio broadcasting, television and the rights of translation into foreign languages are strictly reserved.

ISBN 978-0-573-11652-0
www.samuelfrench.co.uk
www.samuelfrench.com

For Amateur Production Enquiries

United Kingdom and World
excluding north america
plays@samuelfrench.co.uk
020 7255 4302/01

Each title is subject to availability from Samuel French, depending upon country of performance.

CAUTION: Professional and amateur producers are hereby warned that THE SCANDALOUS AFFAIR OF MR KETTLE AND MRS MOON is subject to a licensing fee. Publication of this play does not imply availability for performance. Both amateurs and professionals considering a production are strongly advised to apply to the appropriate agent before starting rehearsals, advertising, or booking a theatre. A licensing fee must be paid whether the title is presented for charity or gain and whether or not admission is charged.

The Professional Rights in this play are controlled by United Agents LLP, 12-26 Lexington St, Soho, London W1F 0LE.

No one shall make any changes in this title for the purpose of production. No part of this book may be reproduced, stored in a retrieval system, or transmitted in any form, by any means, now known or yet to be invented, including mechanical, electronic, photocopying, recording, videotaping, or otherwise, without the prior written permission of the publisher. No one shall upload this title, or part of this title, to any social media websites.

The right of J.B. Priestley to be identified as author of this work has been asserted in accordance with Section 77 of the Copyright, Designs and Patents Act 1988.

MR KETTLE AND MRS MOON

Produced at the Duchess Theatre, London, on the 1st September 1955, with the following cast of characters—

(in the order of their appearance)

GEORGE KETTLE	*Clive Morton*
MRS TWIGG, the housekeeper	*Phyllis Morris*
MONICA TWIGG, Mrs Twigg's daughter	*Wendy Craig*
ALDERMAN HARDACRE	*Julian Somers*
SUPERINTENDENT STREET	*Richard Warner*
DELIA MOON	*Frances Rowe*
HENRY MOON, her husband	*Raymond Francis*
MR CLINTON	*Beckett Bould*
DR GRENOCK	*John Moffatt*

The Play directed by TONY RICHARDSON
Setting by PAUL MAYO

SYNOPSIS OF SCENES

The action of the Play passes in the living-room of George Kettle's flat in Brickmill, a town in the Midlands, on a wet Monday in November

ACT I
Morning

ACT II
Afternoon

ACT III
Early evening

Time—the present

MR KETTLE AND MRS MOON

ACT I

SCENE—*The living-room of George Kettle's flat in Brickmill, a town in the Midlands. A wet Monday morning in November.*

The flat consists of the ground floor of a solid Victorian villa. The living-room has a door R *leading to the hall, a door down* L *to the kitchen and an arch in an alcove up* R *giving access to the bedroom. A large window in a deep bay up* L *overlooks the street. The fireplace is presumed to be in the "fourth wall". The room is furnished in a shabby-comfortable masculine style. There is a big sofa* RC *with a small table* L *of it; an easy chair* LC; *a dining-table with two chairs in the window bay; a cabinet for drinks down* L; *a powerful radiogram upstage of the door down* R, *and a business-like desk and telephone up* C. *At night the room is lit by a standard lamp* R *of the desk, and electric-candle wall-brackets* R *and* L. *The switch for the brackets is below the door* L.

(See the Ground Plan and Photograph of the Scene)

When the CURTAIN *rises* GEORGE KETTLE, *an attractive man in his forties, is discovered sitting on the sofa, at the* L *end, finishing his breakfast which is set on a small collapsible table. He is in dark formal clothes. The rain can be heard outside the window. There are some lights on. With a fixed resigned melancholy look, which never changes, Kettle takes a last sip of tea, wipes his mouth and then folds his napkin, rises and goes into the hall for his hat, coat, umbrella and scarf. He re-enters and places the umbrella on the dining-room table and his hat on the settee table, and throws his coat over the back of the sofa. He puts on his scarf and coat, picks up his hat and goes to the mirror and adjusts the hat—he brushes some specks off his coat, picks up the papers, switches off the lights, and goes out. We hear the slam of the outer door off. It is important that he should perform every action very smoothly and carefully, and without moving a muscle of his face.*

Just after the slam, MRS TWIGG, *a mournful-looking working woman in her fifties, enters* R *and immediately switches on the radio, from which there comes the sound of a very noisy cinema organ. She takes the breakfast tray and the small folding table on which it was placed into the kitchen, returning at once with a duster. She begins dusting in a sketchy routine fashion. The telephone rings. She tries to answer it but the radio organ is making too much noise. Putting down the receiver by the side of the telephone, she goes to switch off the radio. But when she picks up the receiver again, shouting "Hello—Hello!" clearly the caller has rung off. She now switches on the radio again, but just as she has moved a step or two away from it, the telephone rings again. This time she switches off the radio first, then answers the telephone.*

MRS TWIGG (*into the telephone*) Yes it is—but he isn't here . . . I don't know . . . What name? . . . Hardacre? All right, Mr Hardacre. (*She puts down the receiver and continues with her work. After a few moments, the telephone rings again. She answers it*) Yes—this is Mr Kettle's flat . . . No, he isn't. He's at the bank, same as usual . . . (*Surprised*) You *are* the bank? Well then, I don't know where he is . . . All I can tell you is he had his breakfast same as usual and set off same as usual . . . No, he didn't seem any different . . . Well, I'll be going home soon—I don't give him his lunch on Mondays, 'cos I have my washing to do at home . . . Yes, I could leave him a note. (*She replaces the receiver and continues with her work. She moves to the window, closes it, then switches on the wall-brackets by the switch below the door* L)

(*The telephone rings*)

(*She moves to the telephone and lifts the receiver. Into the telephone*) Yes, it is—but he isn't here . . . I don't know. Bank's just rung up to ask where he was, and I told 'em I couldn't say . . . What name? . . . Hardacre? . . . All right, Mr Hardacre. (*She replaces the receiver, then moves to the sofa and dusts it*)

(*The sound of the front door closing and of cymbals being clashed is heard off* L.

GEORGE KETTLE *enters* L. *He carries a box containing a child's shooting game, and a drumstick. He moves to the easy chair* LC, *puts the box, his hat and the drumstick on it. He then removes his coat*)

(*Surprised*) Mr Kettle? What's the matter? Have you been taken bad?

KETTLE. No, I've been taken good. (*He hits his hat with the drumstick*)

MRS TWIGG (*puzzled*) How do you mean?

KETTLE. Never mind, Mrs Twigg.

(KETTLE *exits to the hall and hangs his coat on the hall-stand*)

MRS TWIGG. Bank's been asking for you. So has Mr Hardacre —Hardacre's Stores, I suppose?

KETTLE (*off*) That's the chap.

MRS TWIGG. But didn't you go to the bank the same as usual?

KETTLE (*off*) No.

MRS TWIGG. But you set off the same as usual.

(KETTLE *enters from the hall. He carries a pair of cymbals*)

KETTLE (*crossing to Mrs Twigg*) After that it stopped being the same as usual. (*He clashes the cymbals in her face, then puts them on the*

To face page 2—Mr Kettle and Mrs Moon

Photograph by Wilfred Newton

table L *of the sofa and crosses to the arch up* R) Now I'm going to change these clothes.

MRS TWIGG (*puzzled*) Why, Mr Kettle?

KETTLE (*stopping and speaking over his shoulder*) Because I don't like them, Mrs Twigg.

(KETTLE *exits to the bedroom.* MRS TWIGG *looks uncertainly after him*)

MRS TWIGG (*calling*) If you're not feeling well, Mr Kettle, I think you ought to say so.

KETTLE (*off*) I'm feeling fine.

MRS TWIGG. But you can't be—coming back like this . . .

KETTLE (*off*) Never felt better.

MRS TWIGG (*after a pause; worried*) But what about the bank?

KETTLE (*off*) What about it?

MRS TWIGG (*moving to the arch*) Well, they're asking for you.

(*There is no reply*)

(*After a pause*) They don't know where you are. You'll have to let 'em know, won't you?

KETTLE (*off*) No.

(*The telephone rings.* MRS TWIGG *moves to the telephone*)

(*Off. He shouts*) Don't answer it, Mrs Twigg. Just take the receiver off and put it down.

(MRS TWIGG, *bewildered, lifts the telephone receiver to stop it ringing, and lays the receiver on the desk*)

MRS TWIGG (*after a pause*) I suppose you know what you're doing, Mr Kettle?

KETTLE (*off*) Yes, I know what I'm doing. What are *you* doing?

MRS TWIGG. Just tidying up. I like to get back home soon on Mondays.

KETTLE (*off*) Off you go, then.

MRS TWIGG. There's no lunch here for you, y'know, Mr Kettle. Don't forget you always have it at the club on Mondays. (*She dusts the desk*) I suppose I could nip out an' get you something?

(KETTLE *enters from the bedroom. He is now loosely and comfortably dressed, in old corduroy trousers and a jersey, or whatever the actor prefers. He is in his socks. He looks quite different from the formal type who went into the bedroom: a relaxed, free-and-easy man*)

KETTLE. No, thank you, Mrs Twigg. (*He moves to the desk and picks up the receiver. Into the telephone*) Good-bye. (*He puts the receiver on the desk. To Mrs Twigg*) Now you go home. (*During the following dialogue he sits on the sofa, puts on a pair of casual shoes* which are on the floor in front of the sofa, then takes his pipe and tobacco from his pocket and fills and lights his pipe)

(MRS TWIGG *watches anxiously, clearly baffled by Kettle's conduct*)

MRS TWIGG. What about the telephone?
KETTLE. That's all right.
MRS TWIGG. But nobody can talk to you if it's like that. It's *engaged* all the time.
KETTLE (*rising and crossing to the cabinet down* L) Probably it likes to be engaged. (*He pours a whisky and soda for himself*)

(MRS TWIGG, *puzzled, stares at Kettle, then notices the parcel*)

MRS TWIGG (*moving down* C) What is this, sir?
KETTLE. A shooting game.
MRS TWIGG. A shooting game?
KETTLE. I happened to see it in the toyshop window—so I bought it. You shoot at jungle animals and knock them over. I had one—oh—thirty-five years ago—and it seemed to me about time I had another one. (*He sips his drink*)
MRS TWIGG (*looking disapprovingly at the drink*) Mr Kettle, I don't want to say anything I oughtn't—but I must tell you straight I don't like to see you drinking like this in the morning.
KETTLE. Jolly good health! (*He drinks and puts his glass on the table* L *of the sofa, then crosses to the easy chair*)
MRS TWIGG. It isn't right. You don't know what it'll lead to. You're known to be one of the steadiest and best-respected men in Brickmill . . .
KETTLE (*picking up the bowler hat and drumstick and handing them to Mrs Twigg*) Mrs Twigg, never mind about that. Tell me something. Do you like Brickmill? (*He unties the string of the box*)
MRS TWIGG. Well, I've lived here all my life—and . . .
KETTLE (*cutting in*) Now give me a plain answer. *Do you like it?*
MRS TWIGG. No, not much. But we have to put up with it.
KETTLE. Have we?
MRS TWIGG (*surprised*) Well, haven't we?
KETTLE. No. (*To avoid further argument. Gently but firmly*) Now, off you go, Mrs Twigg.
MRS TWIGG (*putting the drumstick on the table* L *of the sofa; a routine question*) Same time in the morning, I suppose, Mr Kettle?
KETTLE (*considering this*) I don't know.
MRS TWIGG (*astonished*) You don't know?
KETTLE. No. Perhaps I shan't be here.
MRS TWIGG. Why, where are you going?
KETTLE (*without emphasis*) I don't know. I haven't any plans. I don't want to have any plans. I'm tired of plans.
MRS TWIGG. You're in a queer state of mind, aren't you, Mr Kettle?

Act I   MR KETTLE AND MRS MOON   5

KETTLE (*thoughtfully*) No, I don't think so, Mrs Twigg.
MRS TWIGG. Perhaps you'll feel better in the morning. Anyhow, I'll come at the usual time. (*She hesitates*) You wouldn't like a nice cup of tea and then a nice lie down, would you?
KETTLE. No, I wouldn't. But you would, wouldn't you? (*Almost coaxingly*) Now, why don't *you* have a nice cup of tea and then a nice lie down?
MRS TWIGG (*wistfully*) I wish I could.
KETTLE. Why not, then?
MRS TWIGG (*severely*) I've too much to do—Monday an' all. Really—I'm surprised at you, Mr Kettle.

(KETTLE *takes his bowler hat from Mrs Twigg*)

Where would we be if everybody started behaving like that?
KETTLE. I don't know. But where are we now? Good morning, Mrs Twigg.
MRS TWIGG (*disapprovingly*) Good *morning*, Mr Kettle.

(MRS TWIGG *crosses and exits to the kitchen.* KETTLE *kicks his bowler hat off through the arch up* R, *then opens the box and sets up the game on the easy chair. The game consists of cardboard lions, tigers, etc. that can be knocked over by rubber-tipped darts fired from little spring pistols. He then tries his hand and shoots three times from various positions.*

MONICA TWIGG *enters* L. *She is a girl of eighteen, dressed in cheap finery, and a rather absurd mixture at the moment of cheap glamour and the woe-begone bedraggled. She wears a raincoat and head-scarf*)

MONICA (*calling as she enters*) Ma! Ma! (*She sees Kettle*) Oh—Mr Kettle.
KETTLE. Yes. You're Mrs Twigg's daughter?
MONICA (*crossing to* C) That's right. Monica. Isn't my mother here?
KETTLE. No, you've just missed her.
MONICA. I thought I might do. But I didn't think you'd be here. Aren't you supposed to be at the bank all day?
KETTLE. Yes. But this morning I'm big-game hunting instead. (*He indicates the game*)
MONICA (*astonished*) Why—that's just a kid's game.
KETTLE. Yes, but I wanted to try it again.
MONICA (*amused*) You don't mean instead of going to the bank?
KETTLE. Yes, I do. But what about you?
MONICA (*moving to* L *of the sofa; confidentially*) I've just got the push again—right off, beginning of the week. The manageress took one look at me—she was right out of temper of course, everybody is on a wet Monday morning—an' she says, "I thought I told you last Friday we didn't want you." So I says,

"Well, I thought you didn't mean it," I says. So she says, "Well, I mean it now an' you go an' get your card," she says. (*She breaks off and looks enquiringly at Kettle*) Well, if I'm going to stay here talking any longer, I'd like to take my coat off an' dry it. But, of course, I'll go if you like. Only it's no use standing here in a wet coat.

KETTLE. Take it off and dry it then.

MONICA (*crossing to the kitchen door*) Okay. It'll dry quickest in the kitchen.

(MONICA *exits to the kitchen.* KETTLE *picks up his glass and sips his drink.*

MONICA *re-enters from the kitchen. She has removed her raincoat and head-scarf and is dressed in a skimpy frock that emphasizes her youthful but fairly full figure, of which she is highly conscious. She has done her best, in this brief time, to make herself look attractive*)

(*She notices Kettle's drink*) I'll bet that's whisky.

KETTLE. It is.

MONICA (*perching herself on the back of the sofa*) You wouldn't like to give me some, I suppose?

KETTLE. No, I shouldn't.

MONICA. I've had some, you know, more than once—out with chaps, though I don't really fancy it. (*She puts her leg up on to the back of the sofa*) I'm more for cocktails. But why wouldn't you give me any whisky? You're not mean, are you?

KETTLE (*thoughtfully*) I don't know—yet. I haven't really started exploring myself. But I'm dead against letting you have any whisky. How old are you? (*He moves to Monica and removes her leg from the back of the sofa*)

MONICA. Eighteen.

KETTLE. You're far too young. (*He continues round the sofa, crosses and picks up a pistol and a dart*) It's wasted on anybody under thirty, in my opinion. By the way, aren't you always changing jobs?

MONICA. That's right. I'll bet my mother's told you that, hasn't she? Trust her! She gets right fed up with me. But I tell her what does it matter. You might as well have a change. One thing's as good as another here in Brickmill. (*She indicates the game*) How do you do this?

KETTLE. I'll show you. (*He goes to* R *of the sofa and fires a dart*) Now you have a try. (*He hands a pistol and dart to Monica*) What do you want to do, Monica?

(*During* MONICA'*s following speech, she fires twice*)

MONICA (*confidentially*) I'd like to be a model—or on television—or a film star. And if I can't be one of them, something with some glamour in it; I don't care what I do—it's all the same. (*Dreamily*) I want to have my photo taken at a night club—

wearing a backless evening gown—holding a glass of champagne wine—"Miss Monica Twigg seen at the Caffy de Paris"—it'll say underneath. And I'd keep flying to places—like they all do—Rome and New York and Hollywood.

KETTLE. You'd probably get tired of flying to places.

MONICA. Well, if I did—I'd pack it up. "Monica Twigg resting in the country"—it 'ud say underneath the photo. Or I'd be wearing a bathing costume at Cap What's-it—where they all go. And I've got as good a figure as most of 'em—better than some. I've had trouble enough with it already—chaps pawing me about—it's got me the sack twice—but so far that's all it has got me. (*She fires again*)

KETTLE. Don't you want to get married?

(MONICA *puts the pistol on the table* L *of the sofa, collects the darts and sets up the animals*)

MONICA. Not in Brickmill, I don't—no fear. It's murder here. What about you, Mr Kettle?

KETTLE. What about me?

MONICA (*moving* C) My mother says you never seem to have any girls here. And you're not married. Don't you go in for sex?

KETTLE. I seem to have been off it for some time, Monica. I was married once, but it didn't work. That was before I came to Brickmill. (*He fires*)

MONICA. Bank send you to different places, I suppose?

KETTLE. Yes, you move around.

MONICA. Well, you picked a bloody awful place when you came here, I must say. As soon as my brother Ted's done his National Service, I'm off . . .

KETTLE. "Miss Monica Twigg boards the bus for Birmingham"—it'll say underneath the photograph.

MONICA (*moving above the table* L *of the sofa; giggling appreciatively*) You're a bit livelier than I thought you'd be, Mr Kettle.

(KETTLE *lies on the sofa and prepares to fire*)

You don't look bad either, dressed like that.

(*The front door bell rings off*)

Somebody at the door.

KETTLE. Can't help that.

MONICA. Aren't you going to answer it?

KETTLE. No. If anybody really wants to see me, he must walk in.

(*There is a sharp knock at the door* L.

ALDERMAN HARDACRE *bursts in* L. *He is a severe-looking elderly man, dressed in a rather old-fashioned dark business style. He is very angry.* KETTLE *fires as Hardacre enters*)

HARDACRE (*crossing to* c) Look here, Kettle—what's happening? They told me at the bank you must be ill.
KETTLE (*mildly*) Well, I'm not.
HARDACRE. So it seems. What on earth are you doing?
KETTLE (*blandly*) I'm playing the "Jungle Shooting Game" with Miss Monica Twigg. Miss Twigg—Alderman Hardacre—Jungle Shooting Game.
MONICA (*impressed*) Hardacre's Stores?
HARDACRE. Yes, young woman—and a very busy man. I don't know what you're supposed to be doing here, but I'll be much obliged if you'll leave us—unless of course you're living here. (*He eyes Monica suspiciously*)
MONICA. Here—here—none o' that. I came to tell my mother, who works for Mr Kettle, I'd got the sack.
HARDACRE. That wouldn't surprise me.
MONICA. I've had the sack from your Stores, too, in my time. And not sorry, either. You've got some stinkers there, let me tell you.
HARDACRE (*angrily*) How d'you mean—stinkers?
MONICA. I could tell you a thing or two.
KETTLE (*helpfully*) She probably could, you know, too.
HARDACRE (*removing his hat*) I wouldn't listen to a word a girl of that type had to say. And if you've any sense, Kettle, you won't. Or let anybody catch you playing silly children's games with her. A man in your position . . .
MONICA (*over the back of the sofa*) I think I'll pop round to the Labour Exchange—an' see what's doing. (*She crosses to the kitchen door*) Bye-bye, Mr Kettle.
KETTLE. Bye-bye, Monica.
HARDACRE. Now, look here, Kettle . . .
MONICA (*to Hardacre; severely*) You want to tell one or two o them old floor managers of yours to keep their hands to themselves. A bit o' fun's all right—but . . .
HARDACRE (*angrily*) Nonsense! Don't tell me . . .
MONICA (*shouting him down*) Nobody can tell you anything, can they? You know it all. So I won't tell you what they call you. But it isn't Hardacre.

(MONICA *exits triumphantly to the kitchen*)

HARDACRE (*staring disapprovingly at Kettle; severely*) If you want my opinion, Kettle, you're more to blame than she is for that piece of impudence. She doesn't know any better. You do. (*He moves to the desk and puts his hat on it*) And you've been encouraging her.
KETTLE (*mildly*) "Jungle Shooting Game"? I don't see any connexion between that and the behaviour of your floor managers, Hardacre. Not that I'd be too hard on them. Monica's obviously charged full of sex—and rather unscrupulous—and when you think of the lives your middle-aged floor managers must lead . . .

HARDACRE (*cutting in*) Don't talk rubbish! (*He moves down* C) My floor managers have all been with me for years—thoroughly decent respectable men . . .
KETTLE (*cutting in*) That's what I'm saying—think of the barren lives . . .
HARDACRE (*angrily*) Drop it. I've wasted enough time this morning. Let's get to business. (*He is severe now rather than wildly angry*) And let me remind you that I represent one of the biggest accounts the London and North Midland Bank has in this district. I could have arranged our Extension Loan directly through the Head Office. But I decided to deal with them through you and our local branch, chiefly as a favour to you. At the time you were very grateful. I call this morning to see you—and what happens? You're not there—and nobody knows if you're ill or gone up to London—or what's going on. I come here—and what are you doing?
KETTLE (*smiling*) Playing the "Jungle Shooting Game".
HARDACRE. With that little—whatever-she-is? And you're not ill.
KETTLE. I never said I was.
HARDACRE (*baffled and angry*) Well, what do you think you're doing? Fooling about—dressed like that—Monday morning. What do you think they'd say if I reported it to your Head Office? And I've half a mind to—I really have.
KETTLE (*sympathetically*) If you feel like that, I think you ought, y'know, Hardacre.
HARDACRE (*amazed*) You think I ought? What's the matter with you, Kettle? Have you been drinking—or what?
KETTLE. I'm having one now. Can I offer you one?
HARDACRE (*angrily*) No, you can't offer me one. I don't drink at any time, and certainly not on Monday morning when I'm up to my eyes in work. As you ought to be, Kettle, and always have been since I've known you.
KETTLE. I'll try to explain.
HARDACRE. I should think so.
KETTLE (*relaxed and easy*) I woke up at the usual time this morning. Had my bath, shaved, put on my usual bank uniform. Had breakfast. Looked at *The Times* and the *Birmingham Post*. Set out for the bank as usual. It was raining—a wet Monday morning in Brickmill. Still, nothing unusual in that. I remembered that you'd be coming in—and some other people with important accounts. I wondered who I'd be lunching with at the club. And then—suddenly—a voice spoke to me.
HARDACRE (*grimly*) I see. A voice spoke to you.
KETTLE. Now you're going to ask me whose voice it was . . .
HARDACRE. No, I'm not. You were talking to yourself.
KETTLE. In a way. But it's rather complicated . . .
HARDACRE. No, it isn't. You told yourself to stay away from the

bank, from your work, and to come back here and drink whisky and play at shooting lions.

KETTLE (*mildly protesting*) I thought you wanted me to try to explain.

HARDACRE (*contemptuously*) Yes—if you've anything sensible to say. But if you haven't, *I'll* say something.

(KETTLE *ignores Hardacre and fires at the animals*)

(*Very angrily*) Will you stop that nonsense and listen to me for a minute? It'll be for your own good.

KETTLE (*rising*) How do you know what my own good is? I don't know much about that myself yet. In fact you might say I'm only just starting to find out.

HARDACRE. I'm an older man than you . . .

KETTLE. I'm only about an hour old.

HARDACRE (*shouting*) Stop that!

KETTLE. Alderman Hardacre, for the last three years I've been tormented by a desire to throw something at you. And now—unless you clear out at once—I'm going to do it. (*He looks around for something to throw*)

(HARDACRE *moves hastily to the desk and picks up his hat*)

A man ought to keep something handy for times like this. One of those custard pies they used to have in the old comic films.

HARDACRE (*crossing to the door* L *and turning*) I'm going. But you realize I came here to discuss important bank business. And this is what I get. Very well, I'm going to ring up your district Head Office.

(HARDACRE *exits* L. KETTLE, *unperturbed, hums a tune, crosses to the radiogram and puts on a record of Borodin's Polovtsian Dances from Prince Igor, after one or two false starts getting the third theme starting with the heavy drum. He turns it on at full blast, then collects his drumstick and experiments happily, trying the stick on various plant pots, etc. Finally, he sits on the sofa and uses the coal scuttle as a drum. He is delightfully absorbed in this.*

SUPERINTENDENT STREET *enters* L. *He is a heavily built man in his fifties. He is astonished at what he sees and hears*)

STREET (*shouting*) Mr Kettle! Mr Kettle!

(KETTLE *sees Street, rises, moves to the radiogram and switches it off.* STREET *crosses to* C)

KETTLE (*crossing to* R *of Street*) Hello, Superintendent.

STREET (*reproachfully*) I rang and knocked but couldn't make you hear, Mr Kettle. I couldn't think what was going on in here. Is there something the matter with your coal scuttle?

KETTLE. I'm using it as a big drum.

STREET. A big drum?

KETTLE. Yes, a big drum. I've always wanted to join in those

ACT I   MR KETTLE AND MRS MOON   11

dances from *Prince Igor*—but never got round to it before. You wouldn't like to try putting in the drum bits while I do the cymbals, would you?
STREET (*severely*) I've something better to do this morning, Mr Kettle, even if you haven't.
KETTLE (*sitting on the sofa at the left end*) No, I haven't, not at the moment.
STREET (*suspiciously*) I called at the bank—and they said I might find you here. Off-colour, are you?
KETTLE (*smiling*) No. I'm on-colour.
STREET. What?
KETTLE. On colour.
STREET (*suspiciously*) Are you all right, Mr Kettle?
KETTLE. I'm fine, Superintendent. How are you?
STREET (*not liking this*) Busy. So I'll come to the point. You'll remember you wrote to us about our parking regulations at your bank corner. You asked if we couldn't see our way to modifying them a bit for the convenience of your customers. Especially on Tuesdays and Saturday mornings—remember?
KETTLE. Superintendent, I'll be frank with you. I don't care.
STREET (*astonished*) You don't care?
KETTLE. Not a rap. Let 'em all park there—or run 'em all in for parking there—just as you please.
STREET (*aggrieved*) It's not a question of just as I please, Mr Kettle. Don't get that into your head. I carry out my instructions, that's all.
KETTLE. You don't sound very happy about it.
STREET. Happy about it. Why should I be happy about it?
KETTLE. But who *is* happy about it?
STREET (*exasperated*) I don't know what you're talking about. Happy about *what*?
KETTLE. Well—about parking near the bank and Alderman Hardacre's loan for his extension, and the way his floor managers behave to girls, and Monica Twigg always getting the sack and Mrs Twigg wanting to get home early on Mondays . . .
STREET (*exasperated*) What *is* all this?
KETTLE (*earnestly*) Almost everything that goes on really, isn't it? And I say—who *is* happy about it? Who is it who's enjoying it all?
STREET (*moving behind the sofa and leaning over the back; confidentially*) Oh—you're feeling like that, are you? Well, I'll admit there've been times when I've had one of them days that go on for ever—and everybody you have anything to do with seems half daft with fuss and worry and vexation—I've asked myself that sort of question. Tried it on the wife, too, when at last I got home, but she could never see what I was driving at, having a very female point of view.
KETTLE. It's not quite that, Superintendent. I tried to tell

Hardacre that I heard a voice this morning, just before I got to the bank. Now that voice, I think, belonged to me as I am now and spoke to him—that is, to me as I was then—and it simply said, "Why, George?" Just that—"Why, George?" And I said, "Do you mean all this—going to the bank on a wet Monday in Brickmill?" And the voice said, "Yes. What's it all for? And how long's it going on?"

STREET. I see. (*He moves* L *of the sofa*) And how long have these voices been going on, Mr Kettle?

KETTLE. No, no. That won't do. One voice. Just this morning. And really—you must grasp this, Superintendent—make an effort now—really *my* voice. I—the man who's talking to you now—asked the question.

STREET (*humouring*) Where's the other one then?

KETTLE. He's gone.

STREET (*clearly humouring Kettle*) Now let's get this straight. The George Kettle who was the manager of the Brickmill branch of the London and North Midland Bank has gone—just vanished.

KETTLE. Yes. That was easy. He was only a sort of ghost.

STREET. Well, I don't know. Seemed a solid dependable kind of chap the three years or so I've known him.

KETTLE. I dare say.

STREET. Well respected in the town. That doesn't suggest a sort of ghost.

KETTLE. Unless it's a ghost town. Have you ever read about those ghost towns near Death Valley in California? They still have railway stations, streets, hotels, shops, banks, houses—but no people, no life there. Now perhaps Brickmill is another kind of ghost town. You're a solid dependable sort of chap, but suddenly you wake up in the main street and you see there isn't anything real.

STREET. But you're the one who woke up.

KETTLE. Yes—I didn't put that very clearly. I woke up and took over—and your solid dependable chap vanished.

STREET. I've got it now. Well, I hope you're as friendly as the other George Kettle was.

KETTLE. More friendly, I'd say.

STREET. Then you wouldn't object to doing me a small favour?

KETTLE. I hope not, Superintendent. What is it?

STREET (*earnestly*) Just promise me you won't go out until you see me again. You won't be missing anything. It's a nasty day. You're snug in here. I feel you'd enjoy yourself a lot better staying indoors. What do you say? Just as a favour?

KETTLE (*rising*) As a matter of fact, I'd no intention of going out again this morning. But, as you insist upon it, I'll stay in this afternoon, too. But I may have to go out before the shops close, you know.

STREET. Yes, yes, I'll be back before then. (*He crosses to the door* L) Well—er . . .

(KETTLE *picks up one of the pistols and moves up* L *of the table* L *of the sofa*)

KETTLE (*threatening Street with the pistol; casually*) By the way, Superintendent, I'd like to make one thing clear before you go. Because it might save you a good deal of trouble.

STREET (*moving slowly and cautiously to Kettle*) And what's that?

KETTLE (*smiling*) I haven't gone mad, you know.

STREET (*with false heartiness*) Bless my heart and soul, Mr Kettle, I've never imagined such a thing for a minute. You're as sane as I am.

KETTLE. I'm saner than you are. *Now*.

STREET (*heartily*) I wouldn't be surprised. (*He suddenly disarms Kettle and realizes the pistol is a toy. He notices the shooting game, and anxious to change the subject, points to it*) Now what's that you've got there?

KETTLE. The "Jungle Shooting Game". Like to try it? (*He loads the pistol for Street, then loads the other for himself*)

(STREET *sits on the sofa, at the right end.* KETTLE *sits on the left arm of the sofa and during the ensuing dialogue is always prevented from firing by* STREET *taking the pistol from him after he has reloaded it*)

STREET. I used to be a bit of a marksman at one time—but it's years ago. Don't suppose I can do anything with these things. Now then. I'll have a go at that lion first. Never thought I'd do a bit of lion shooting on a wet Monday morning in Brickmill.

KETTLE (*gravely*) No—you owe that to me.

STREET. I do indeed. (*When he shoots, he must appear to shoot very well; if necessary this can be easily faked. He is very pleased with himself*) Down he goes! And another of 'em. (*He names the particular animals as he knocks them down*) Some slaughter in the jungle this morning, Mr Kettle.

KETTLE. But no screams—no blood—no agony—no life ebbing out.

(*The front door bell rings off*)

STREET. Your door, isn't it? (*He rises*) Now don't you bother about this, Mr Kettle. Ten to one it's somebody wanting me— and if it isn't, I can deal with 'em. (*He crosses to the door* L) You don't want to trouble yourself about people this morning.

(STREET *exits* L. KETTLE *rises and packs up the shooting game in its box.*

STREET *re-enters* L *and moves to* L *of the easy chair*)

Well, it was for you, not for me. Mrs Henry Moon. She'd been to the bank—and they'd told her to try here. She's the chairman of some fund committee—Infirmary Wireless Fund, isn't it?—that you're treasurer of. But I did say you wouldn't be up to adding her Wireless Fund figures for her this morning—so she popped off. She'd come in her red sports car—so it was no trouble. I did right, didn't I? You wouldn't want to be bothered with her this morning, would you?

KETTLE (*moving to Street; thoughtfully*) Why should Mrs Moon have a red sports car?

STREET. Why shouldn't she? Henry Moon can afford to keep two or three cars. And a nippy little car like that is just right for a woman to drive herself—shopping and so forth.

KETTLE (*still thoughtfully*) Yes, but why should a cold severe woman like Mrs Moon choose a bright red sports car. Something's wrong.

STREET (*heartily*) Oh—they all have their little fancies. Well, I'm off. And just you enjoy yourself here—dances, drums, and all—till I get back. Don't forget your promise.

(STREET *exits* L. KETTLE *puts the game on the dining-table up* L, *then moves to the desk and looks up a number in the telephone directory pad, humming the tune of the record to himself. He lifts the receiver and dials a number*)

KETTLE (*into the telephone*) Moon and Francis? . . . Is Mr Henry Moon there, please? . . . George Kettle . . . Yes, I think it's *very* important. (*He waits*) Mr Moon? . . . This is George Kettle . . . No, it won't take a minute. It's about that red sports car that Mrs Moon drives . . . No, there's nothing gone wrong with it that I know of . . . That's not the point. What I want to know is this. Did you give it to her or did she choose it herself? . . . No, I'm not trying to be funny . . . Well, this *is* what I rang you up about . . . Bought it herself, did she? . . . No, it isn't bank business—nothing wrong there . . . Damned impudence? Oh, I don't know, Mr Moon. Fascinating name, by the way. Perhaps that's why she married you. (*He replaces the receiver to break the call, then removes the receiver and lays it on the desk. He has the air of a man who has just done a good job. He moves to the radiogram and switches on the record. He then collects the cymbals and drumstick and sits on the sofa. He attempts to beat time on the coal scuttle and clash the cymbals at the same time. He ends by putting the cymbals on his feet*)

(DELIA MOON *enters* L. *She is a good-looking but severe-looking woman in her middle or later thirties, well but severely dressed. The look of cold severity is increased by her wearing diamond-shaped or similar spectacles. She is clearly rather pleasantly surprised by Kettle's unusual appearance.* KETTLE *finds keeping time to the record too difficult, so removes the cymbals from his feet, rises, crosses to the radiogram and switches off. He turns and sees Delia*)

KETTLE (*crossing to* c) Hello, Mrs Moon.
DELIA (*moving to* L *of Kettle*) Good morning, Mr Kettle. I did ring and knock . . .
KETTLE. Too much noise here—yes.
DELIA. You look quite different in those clothes. What are you trying to do?
KETTLE. I'm trying to join in this thingummy dance from *Prince Igor*, but it's very difficult to work both the big drum—that's the coal scuttle—and the cymbals. It needs two people. We might try in a minute.
DELIA (*not unpleasantly but not committing herself*) Oh—might we?
KETTLE (*gravely*) I'm appealing now to the bit of you that chose the red sports car.
DELIA. I see. But let's talk about you for a minute, shall we? I've had three different accounts of you this morning. I went to the bank and they said you were probably ill. Then Alderman Hardacre came in—in a filthy temper—and said you must have been drinking for days. I came here, and Superintendent Street said I'd better not come in because you seemed to him more than half dotty. So I pretended to drive away, but as soon as I knew he'd gone, I hurried back, dying of curiosity. You don't seem to me ill, drunk or dotty.
KETTLE. I'm not. Those fellows don't understand, though I did my best with the Superintendent. By the way, I rang up your husband just now about the red sports car.
DELIA (*amused*) You rang up Henry. Why?
KETTLE. I had to know whether he'd given it to you or you'd chosen it yourself.
DELIA. I'll bet he was furious.
KETTLE. He was, after I'd told him it wasn't bank business.
DELIA. But why did you want to know, Mr Kettle?
KETTLE. When the Superintendent came back from shooing you off, he mentioned your red sports car, and I suddenly wondered how you came to have such a thing. Quite unlike my idea of you. And perhaps my idea of you was wrong. (*He collects the drumstick*)
DELIA. And that's why you risked asking me to bang the coal scuttle for you?
KETTLE. Yes. But you can have the cymbals if you like.
DELIA (*taking the drumstick*) No, I'll be on the big drum. But not for long, mind you.
KETTLE. Don't do it at all if you're against it.
DELIA. No, let's get it over with. You won't be happy until you hear what it sounds like, will you?
KETTLE. No. And that's the first sensible thing anybody's said to me this morning. I'm very glad I wondered about that red sports car. (*He moves to* R *of the sofa and picks up the cymbals*) Now

then—you remember how it goes—"boom da da—boom da da—boom da da"?

DELIA. Yes—but I'll miss the very first *boom*, you know, because it'll have started before I know it's started, if you see what I mean. (*She sits on the sofa at the right end*)

KETTLE (*moving to the radiogram and switching it on*) Yes, of course. (*He moves to* R *of the sofa*)

(*They have a go.* DELIA *hits the coal scuttle while* KETTLE *clashes the cymbals. During Delia's following speech, to enable the words to be heard, the music is reduced in volume and increased at the end of the speech by off-stage control*)

DELIA (*after a dozen bars or so; shouting*) Just a minute! Stop it! Don't you think it would be better if I bashed a cymbal with this stick when it gets to the top—"diddle-diddle-diddle-diddle"—that part? You hold a cymbal out—and I'll bash it—um?

KETTLE. It's an idea. We'll try it again, then.

(*They have a good happy go now.* DELIA *hits the cymbal on the fifth bar, etc.*)

DELIA (*shouting*) That's enough. Can't take any more just now.

(KETTLE *puts the cymbals on the sofa, crosses to the radiogram and switches it off*)

KETTLE (*moving* C) Thank you very much, Mrs Moon. I think I've wanted to do that for years. Like a drink?

DELIA (*with mock severity*) I'm not in the habit of drinking in the morning, Mr Kettle. (*She puts the drumstick on the sofa seat*)

KETTLE (*collecting his glass*) You're not in the habit of playing the coal scuttle in the morning, either, are you, Mrs Moon? (*He crosses to the cabinet down* L) So never mind about habits. Would you like a drink? I'm having one.

DELIA. All right, then.

KETTLE. I'm having a whisky. But there's sherry, if you'd prefer it.

DELIA. Yes, please.

(KETTLE *takes a decanter of sherry from the cabinet cupboard, pours a glass of sherry for Delia and a whisky and soda for himself*)

I went to the bank to ask you about the accounts of the Infirmary Wireless Fund. Are you interested?

KETTLE (*pleasantly*) Not at all.

DELIA. Isn't that a shocking thing for a bank manager to say, Mr Kettle?

KETTLE. It's an impossible thing for a bank manager to say, Mrs Moon. (*He crosses to her and gives her the drink, then raises his own glass*) Boom-da-da! (*He drinks*)

DELIA. Diddle-diddle! (*She sips her sherry*)
KETTLE. But I'm no longer a bank manager. I stopped this morning—about twenty-five past nine.
DELIA. Just like that?
KETTLE (*moving to* L *of the easy chair*) It took about three seconds. There I was, on my way, nearly there in fact—and suddenly a voice said, "Why, George?" "Why! What's it all for? And how long's it going on?" I couldn't reply. So I packed it up. And that's why they all think I'm ill, drunk or barmy. But I'm not. I've just packed it up, that's all.
DELIA. And what are you going to do now?
KETTLE. Not a good question. Not coming from a coal scuttle drummer and cymbal basher.
DELIA. You're probably right. But women can't help being tremendous planners, you know, Mr Kettle. I take it, you don't know yet what you're going to do?
KETTLE. Yes, I do. I'm just going to be *not* a bank manager. The opposite of what Superintendent Street calls a solid dependable chap. So you'd better ask young Morgan to be your treasurer until they've appointed another manager. I'm sorry in a way, Mrs Moon, because that was the only thing that really brought us together, and up to a point I enjoyed that.
DELIA. Up to what point, Mr Kettle?
KETTLE (*with decision*) No, Mrs Moon.
DELIA. Now why do you say that?
KETTLE. When I turned back this morning, I knew that one of the first things I must do was to stop pretending. I'd had years and years of it—and I'd had enough. Now if you begin asking me personal questions, I'll answer you truthfully—and you mightn't like that. I don't mind offending people I dislike—old Hardacre, for instance—but I don't want to offend you, if I can help it.
DELIA. But perhaps you won't offend me. After all, you said I was very sensible about the *Prince Igor* dance.
KETTLE. You were splendid, Mrs Moon.
DELIA. And in any case—as you ought to realize—you've now raised my curiosity to such a height that I've almost got a temperature.
KETTLE. You look the same as usual.
DELIA. And what's that?
KETTLE. Slightly sub-normal.
DELIA (*putting her glass on the table* L *of the sofa*) If you mean by that, I look cool and rather severe, let me tell you that's the way I try to look—and take quite a lot of trouble about it.
KETTLE. Very well. And this'll answer your question. When we used to meet on the Fund Committee, half-dead or asleep though I was then, I'd spend half the time wondering what it would be like to take off those damned spectacles of yours, ruffle

your hair, change those sensible clothes, put you into frills and nonsense, and make love to you.

DELIA (*rising; gasping a little*) Oh!

KETTLE. That's what I meant when I said I enjoyed meeting you up to a point.

DELIA. Does something like that go on in your mind with most women you meet?

KETTLE. No. Chiefly with you.

DELIA (*with decision*) Well! (*She crosses to the door* L)

KETTLE. What are you going to do now? Fetch the Superintendent?

DELIA. No.

(DELIA *exit* L. KETTLE *makes as if to follow her, then checks himself, crosses to the cabinet down* L, *shrugs and refills his glass. He looks rather miserable. He makes one or two small restless movements, then stops, hearing something. The front door is heard to open, close, and the sound of it being locked, follows.* KETTLE, *surprised and delighted, stares at the door* L.

DELIA *re-enters* L. *She carries a basket of food parcels, and a dress box. She dumps the basket and parcel on the desk, picks up her sherry glass and drains it, then looks at Kettle*)

"Fetch the Superintendent!" That was a stupid thing to say, wasn't it? (*She puts her glass on the table* L *of the sofa*)

KETTLE. Yes. Easily the stupidest thing I've said this morning.

DELIA. Do you think you're the only person in this brute of a town who can stop pretending?

KETTLE. I'm hoping I'm not.

DELIA. Not that *you're* going to take off these damned spectacles of mine, ruffle my hair, change my suitable clothes, and put me into frills and nonsense. But *I am*. (*She picks up the dress box*) Now where's a bedroom? (*She points to the arch up* R) Through there?

KETTLE. Yes, the door at the end.

DELIA. Right.

(DELIA *exits up* R. KETTLE *crosses to the standard lamp and switches it on. He then looks up a number in the telephone directory pad, picks up the receiver and dials a number, humming to himself*)

KETTLE (*into the telephone*) Hardacre's Stores? . . . This is the London and North Midland Bank, wishing to speak to Alderman Hardacre . . . Yes, very urgent . . . (*He now uses a voice unlike his ordinary one*) Alderman Hardacre? . . . Yes, this is the London and North Midland Bank . . . No, it's not about your Extension Loan . . . It's about life—L-I-F-E. We thought you'd like to know that we think it's *wonderful*. Good morning. (*He replaces the receiver to break the call, then lifts the receiver and puts it on the desk.*

He then crosses to the light switch L *and switches off the wall-brackets, changing the lighting so that it is warm and intimate*)

(DELIA *enters from the bedroom. She looks very different. She is wearing some sort of soft loose housecoat; her hair is looser; the spectacles have gone, and she looks an extremely attractive and very feminine creature.* KETTLE *stares at her in astonished admiration*)

DELIA (*crossing to* C *and displaying the housecoat; smiling*) Well?

(KETTLE *moves behind the easy chair* LC)

Is this what you imagined?

KETTLE (*enthusiastically*) No, this is much much better. Crikey —woman—what a transformation. But tell me—which is you— this one or the other one?

DELIA. I don't know. Both probably.

KETTLE. Or somebody different from either.

DELIA. Yes.

KETTLE. Just as I'm not really either a bank manager, a solid dependable, or a purely anti-bank manager type, but probably different from either.

DELIA. Can I have a cigarette?

KETTLE (*crossing to the table* L *of the sofa*) You can. (*He offers her a cigarette from the box on the table*) But there seems something all wrong about this settling down for a smoke—it's an anticlimax.

DELIA (*taking a cigarette*) Yes, but we're both feeling self-conscious.

(KETTLE *lights Delia's cigarette*)

(*She sits in the easy chair* LC) Better to talk for a while—if it's honest talk.

KETTLE. I'll do my best. But remember—I'm new to it. We chaps deceive ourselves, you know. I imagine you don't—as a rule.

DELIA. No. We just indulge in one enormous piece of self-deception—about a father, a lover or husband, a son—and that's all. Now—I know you're not married . . .

KETTLE (*standing* L *of the sofa*) I was. We bust up during the war, when I was in the army. The Pay Corps, by the way—no heroics. She thought I was too dull. And she was right—I was.

DELIA. Did she find an exciting man?

KETTLE. He sells typewriters now in Manchester—and plays golf every weekend. But that proves nothing. He may still be all "a wonder and a wild desire".

DELIA. What I meant to ask was—have you a mistress?

KETTLE. No.

DELIA. I thought all you men had—even in Brickmill.

KETTLE. Some have, some haven't. I'm always being surprised. But then I alternate between believing that people are making illicit love all over the place and concluding that there isn't as much of it as we're apt to think.

DELIA (*amused*) So do I. And just when I think it's one, something happens that seems to prove it's the other.

KETTLE. Yes. How about you and Henry Moon?

DELIA. It doesn't work. The trouble is—I don't even like him any more.

KETTLE. I hardly know him. But he always seems to me a little unreal. (*He transfers the ashtray from the left arm of the sofa to the right arm of the easy chair*) Like a lot of estate agents. They themselves seem as unreal as their advertisements—"charming old-world residence replete with all modern conveniences"—that sort of thing.

DELIA. Yes, Henry's like that. Even if you quarrel, you can't make him stop acting—he won't become real.

KETTLE. Is your cold severe performance for him—or for yourself?

DELIA. A bit of both. He thinks it's smart—and safe. And it's my reply to Brickmill. In another place I mightn't bother keeping it up. Or with another man.

KETTLE. Have you just bought that astonishing thing you're wearing?

DELIA. Yes, I saw it in Morley's—and bought it to wear in secret, just for my own pleasure.

KETTLE. And now for mine.

DELIA. I hope so. There's food in the other parcels—nice greedy food—that I also bought because it was raining and November in Brickmill and I was thirty-six and hadn't a lover. We'll eat it soon. (*She stubs out her cigarette*)

KETTLE. Not yet—I think—don't you? And it isn't raining, it isn't November, we aren't in Brickmill, thirty-six is the perfect age, and you have a lover. Get up, please, Mrs Moon.

DELIA. If you prefer it, Mr Kettle. (*She rises and stands facing Kettle, looking at him*)

KETTLE (*very gently*) You're very beautiful. You're what a man feels life ought to be when he dares to think like a man. For the last year or two, every time I stared at you and wondered, aching a little, I must have known somehow this moment was coming if I dared to meet it. Now I want anything you want, and don't want anything you don't want.

DELIA (*half laughing*) You're very sweet. But all wrong. (*She moves slowly close to him*) You're supposed to be more masterful than that.

KETTLE. Certainly.

KETTLE *takes* DELIA *in his arms and they kiss passionately, but do not hold each other long. They look at each other as—*

the CURTAIN *falls*.

ACT II

SCENE—*The same. Afternoon.*

When the CURTAIN *rises, it is the middle of the afternoon. It is raining. The lights are on and the window curtains are closed. The remains of lunch are on the dining-table, on a folding table-tray below the sofa, and various coffee cups, plates, etc., are scattered around, some on the floor below the sofa. The stage is empty, but* DELIA *enters immediately from the bedroom. She is dressed as she was for her first entrance in Act I, and her housecoat is draped over the back of the sofa. She crosses to the window, opens the curtains, then takes a look at the lunch things scattered around, and with the instinct of a tidy woman, but with a slight move of distaste, begins in a very leisurely fashion to put them together before taking them in the kitchen.* MONICA *enters from the kitchen. She is dressed as before, and is wearing her raincoat, which is rather wet. The two stare curiously at each other.*

DELIA (*standing by the dining-table; surprised*) Oh—good afternoon.

MONICA (*cheerfully*) 'Afternoon.

DELIA (*amused*) Wasn't the back door locked, then?

MONICA. No. Ought it to have been? (*She crosses to* C. *Getting no reply she continues cheerfully*) Well, I wouldn't know, would I?

DELIA (*crossing to* L *of Monica; obviously amused by her*) And I wouldn't know who you are.

MONICA. Monica Twigg. My mother looks after . . .

DELIA (*cutting in*) Yes, yes. He told me.

MONICA. Where *is* Mr Kettle?

DELIA (*waving a hand towards the bedroom*) He's asleep.

MONICA. He's not ill, is he?

DELIA (*with mock gravity*) No. He seemed to me in the best of health.

MONICA (*confidentially*) That's what I thought this morning. My mother said he was ill and I said he wasn't. Just fed up, like me, I said.

DELIA. It can happen to any of us on a wet Monday in Brickmill—can't it?

MONICA. It's a wet Monday here all the week, if you ask me. I think I'll dry my coat in the kitchen.

DELIA. Do. And take these with you, Monica. (*She hands Monica some lunch things from the dining-table*)

(MONICA *exits to the kitchen.* DELIA *stacks the coffee cups, then moves towards the arch up* R.

MONICA *re-enters from the kitchen, without her raincoat, and notices Delia's housecoat on the back of the sofa*)

MONICA (*indicating the housecoat*) Is this yours?

DELIA. Yes. I bought it this morning, just to cheer myself up.

MONICA. I saw it in Morley's window. Can I have a look at it?

DELIA. Yes, of course.

MONICA (*picking up the housecoat*) Smashing! (*She drapes it against herself*) This is what I see myself in—when I've got somewhere. Under the photo it'll say—"Miss Monica Twigg relaxes at home". (*She falls into an ecstatic trance*)

DELIA (*crossing and sitting on the left arm of the easy chair*) A sort of Career Girl, aren't you, Monica?

MONICA (*rather gloomily*) When I can get going. (*She puts the housecoat carefully over the back of the sofa*) Though I can't make up my mind if I ought to go in for bein' a model—or films—television. Did you show this to Mr Kettle?

DELIA. Yes. I thought it might amuse him. Though I came to see him on Hospital Committee business. He's the treasurer.

MONICA (*moving to* R *of the easy chair; darkly*) If you ask me, it's not committee business he wants.

DELIA. Oh?

MONICA (*darkly*) No. What he could do with is—*sex*.

DELIA (*half-laughing*) Monica!

MONICA (*bursting out*) I don't care—I'll bet it's true. I expect you're like my mum who says he doesn't go in for it. She says I've got it on the brain, and that lots of men don't go in for it. Well, all I can say is—every time I get a job they seem to me to be going in for it, good an' proper. The trouble I have with 'em.

DELIA. Yes, I can see you might have, Monica. (*She rises, crosses to the sofa and picks up the housecoat*) Some girls do. But where does Mr Kettle come in? Don't tell me . . .

MONICA (*cutting in: confidentially*) No, he's never made any passes at me. Not so much as one of those looks.

(DELIA *crosses and puts the housecoat on the chair* L *of the dining-table*)

(*She follows Delia up* L) But I saw right off this morning, he's just as fed up as I am—he's in a Rebellious Mood—Mr Kettle is—ready to clear out of Brickmill for good an' all—(*grandly*) to wipe the dust from his shoes. And if he is, then I'm ready to go with him.

(DELIA, *during the ensuing dialogue, collects the remainder of the plates and dishes, piles them on the table-tray, and eventually sits on the left arm of the easy chair.* MONICA *moves and stands* L *of the table* L *of the sofa*)

DELIA. No, Monica, I don't think . . .

Act II   MR KETTLE AND MRS MOON   23

MONICA (*cutting in; with fine sweep*) I'll say to him straight out, "Take me with you, Mr Kettle". Mind you, I'll warn him that he's only a stepping stone in my career. I'd be using him just as he'd be using me.

DELIA. It doesn't sound a very nice arrangement, Monica.

MONICA (*grandly*) I'd be honest with him. He could regard me as a plaything of an idle hour—that's up to him—but all the time I'd be on the look-out for the next stepping stone. Because I'm more for Cold Glamour than just sex. It'll say in the papers, "Miss Monica Twigg laughingly denied any rumours of romance. 'We are just friends,' she said."

DELIA. Who are you with now?

MONICA (*with careless grandeur*) Oh—one of these rich Californian playboys—or Eastern princes.

DELIA. With poor Mr Kettle left far behind?

MONICA (*still in the part*) Just one of those things. That's life, isn't it?

DELIA (*briskly*) Not for most of us, it isn't. Suppose you help me to wash up?

MONICA (*deflated*) Mum'll do it when she comes in tonight. She'd rather. She wouldn't thank us for doing it. She likes to look after Mr Kettle. But I'll bet she doesn't know as much about him as I do.

DELIA. And I'll bet you don't know as much about him as *I* do, Monica. You're much too young. And if I were you, I wouldn't bother about running a career. It takes a lot of hard work and determination. It's much more fun just being nobody.

MONICA. Not in Brickmill it isn't. And I'm sure I'm good at *something*—even if I don't know what it is yet. And how can you know if they don't let you try? And anyhow, I've had enough of this lousy hole.

DELIA. But isn't there any nice boy who's interested in you, Monica?

MONICA. Yes, two or three. Trouble about nice boys is that I'm not interested in *them*. They're so *dull*. And the other sort, who aren't dull, mess you about so much. People think I'm a sexy type—that's how I lose jobs—but I'm not so gone on sex.

DELIA. Give it time. You'll be surprised.

MONICA (*indignantly*) All these pieces in women's mags—they make me mad. All about what you must do to find him and keep him. "Make yourself fresh and dainty for him." And just look what you've got to keep yourself fresh and dainty for.

DELIA (*laughing*) I quite agree. That's why I stopped reading those magazines.

MONICA (*indignantly*) Why don't they have a go at keeping fresh and dainty for *us*? And what d'you get for it all? Your photo in the papers sitting in night clubs? Big cars and airplanes to de luxe hotels? No bloody fear! All you get is four kids, a kitchen full of washing, red hands an' flat feet an' Housewives' Choice. (*She breaks off, then looks hopefully at Delia*) I expect you *do* know Mr Kettle better than I do.

DELIA (*rising and picking up the loaded tray; firmly*) Quite definitely, Monica.

MONICA. Then d'you think he'd just take me to Birmingham—to have late dinner an' wine—an' coffee in the lounge with liq-ures?

DELIA (*firmly*) No, Monica. Mr Kettle is the quiet type—he just doesn't like wild nights in Birmingham.

MONICA (*gloomily*) It'll have to be that buyer at Hardacres then.

DELIA. He sounds much more promising.

MONICA. Only—he's so fat.

DELIA. It's all those late dinners and wine, probably. But that's the type.

(*The front door bell rings urgently off*)

Is that the front door?

MONICA. Yes.

DELIA. See who it is—that's a good girl. Don't let anybody in until I know who it is. Unlock the door and peep out.

MONICA (*crossing to the door* L) Okay. I could do a turn as a maid, couldn't I?

DELIA. Why not?

(MONICA *exits* L.

DELIA *exits with the tray to the kitchen, re-enters, exits with the folding table to the kitchen, then re-enters and moves* C.

MONICA *re-enters from the hall, full of excitement*)

MONICA (*crossing to* L *of Delia*) It's a Mr Moon—an' he says his wife's here. You're not her—are you?

DELIA. Yes.

MONICA (*impressed and delighted*) Oi—this could be getting a bit hot. What shall I tell him?

DELIA (*moving towards the arch up* R) He'd better come in. I'll be back in a minute.

(MONICA *exits* L.

DELIA *exits to the bedroom*.

HENRY MOON *enters* L. MONICA *follows him on*. MOON *is a fairly large, stupid-looking man in his late forties, dressed in the tweedy style of the estate-agent-County-gent. He stares around in surprise*)

MONICA. This way, please.

MOON (*crossing to* C) Nobody here.

MONICA (*handsomely overplaying the maid*) Mrs Moon asked me to tell you, Mr Moon, that she would be with you in a minute. (*She closes the door*)

MOON (*staring at Monica*) Oh—she did, eh?
MONICA. In the meantime, Mr Moon, would you care to be seated? (*She indicates the easy chair*)
MOON (*still surprised*) Oh, yes—certainly. (*He sits in the easy chair, and stares at Monica*)

(MONICA *returns Moon's stare for a few moments, then sits at the left end of the sofa*)

MONICA. Not very pleasant weather we're having, is it, Mr Moon?
MOON (*irritated*) What *is* this?
MONICA. What is what, Mr Moon?
MOON. What's the matter with you, girl? (*He looks in astonishment at Monica*)
MONICA (*solemnly*) You think I'm the maid here, don't you, Mr Moon?
MOON. Well, aren't you?
MONICA (*with immense dignity*) Not at all.
MOON. Oh!
MONICA (*loftily*) As a matter of fact, if you're interested, Mr Moon, I'm an actress—well known in films and television. I'm beginning rehearsals next week for the part of a maid—not a small part, quite important, actually—for a television play. So I thought I'd just try it out, y'know, Mr Moon.
MOON. You—you did, did you? Well, what are you doing here?
MONICA. Trying it out.
MOON. But why should you be trying it out here?
MONICA (*loftily*) Oh—I see what you mean, Mr Moon. Well, I happen to be visiting relations in Brickmill. But, of course, I live in London.
MOON. And how long have you been living in London?
MONICA. Oh—several years. Why?
MOON (*triumphantly*) Because—about a month or two ago, you served me with coffee in the café in Market Street.
MONICA (*rising; annoyed*) Okay—what if I did?
MOON (*rising and moving about the easy chair; indignantly*) Well, why tell me all that stuff about television and being an actress?
MONICA (*moving above the right end of the sofa*) Just hopeless trying to kid you, isn't it?
MOON (*complacently*) Yes.
MONICA (*grimly*) I'll bet.

(DELIA *enters from the bedroom, looking tidy and composed. She wears her spectacles*)

MOON (*acknowledging Delia; without surprise*) Delia.
DELIA (*composedly*) Henry.

Monica (*cheerfully*) Well, I'll say good afternoon, Mr and Mrs Moon.
  (Monica *exits to the kitchen*. Delia *crosses to* c)
  Moon (*moving to* L *of Delia; indignantly*) Tried to stuff me with all kinds of nonsense, that girl. Caught her out at once, though. Made her look silly. Cheeky little devil!
  Delia. She is rather. (*She crosses and sits in the easy chair*)
  Moon. Quite. Bit fishy her being around here, isn't it?
  Delia. No, Henry. She's the daughter of George Kettle's housekeeper.
  Moon (*putting his hat and umbrella on the dining-table*) Oh—is she? Well, Delia, I guessed you were here because I saw your car outside. (*He moves* c) Otherwise I wouldn't have known, of course.
  Delia. No, Henry, you wouldn't.
  Moon. No. Not the least idea you were here before that, naturally. Saw your car outside.
  Delia. Yes, you said that. But what were you doing outside?
  Moon. I came to have a word with Kettle. He's here, isn't he?
  Delia. Yes. In his bedroom.
  Moon. Taken queer?
  Delia. No, he's just asleep.
  Moon (*indignantly*) Asleep? That's a bit much, isn't it?
  Delia. He felt sleepy—after lunch. He gave me lunch here, you know.
  Moon. Any particular reason?
  Delia. We were both hungry.
  Moon. They told me at the bank you'd been asking for him this morning. Hospital Fund business, wasn't it?
  Delia. In the first place, Henry—yes.
  Moon. How do you mean—"in the first place"?
  Delia. That's why I called to see him. What about you?
  Moon. What about me?
  Delia. Why have you called to see him?
  Moon. Oh—well, Kettle rang me up this morning. Told the girl it was very urgent. Then it turned out to be some dam' silly question about you and your car. Sounded fishy to me. Thought the tax people had been sniffling round. But when I lunched at the club, I heard some funny rumours about Kettle. Some very queer tales going round, Delia. Hardacre says he's drinking hard. Somebody else said he was half off his rocker. How did he strike you?
  Delia. He seemed to me fairly sober and quite sane, Henry.
  Moon. He did, did he? But why is he asleep, then?
  Delia. Because he felt sleepy, Henry. I told you.
  Moon (*indignantly*) That's all very well, but he's not the only man who feels sleepy after lunch. What if we all turned in like that?

DELIA. Then you'd all feel less sleepy in the evening.
MOON. You must admit that it 'ud be a bit thick if we all slept after lunch. Besides, what about you, Delia?
DELIA. What about me, Henry?
MOON (*indignantly*) Well—dash it all—I mean to say—a chap oughtn't to give a woman lunch and then just turn in like that. What are *you* supposed to be doing while he's asleep?
DELIA (*thoughtfully*) I think I'm supposed to be washing up.
MOON. Why? Can't the housekeeper wash up?
DELIA. Perhaps she's busy at home. It's Monday, you know, Henry.
MOON (*indignantly*) Of course it's Monday. And that makes the whole thing dam' ridiculous.
DELIA. Why, Henry?
MOON (*crossing above the easy chair to* L *of it; angrily*) Why? Why? Well, look at it. Not the weekend—or holiday time—or anything. But *Monday*. Monday!
DELIA (*dreamily*) Moon Day really—I suppose.
MOON. I dare say—but what does that matter?
DELIA. It ought to matter to you Moons.
MOON (*indignantly*) And that's another thing. Just remember it. When Kettle rang me this morning—and I found it wasn't bank business and gave him a rocket—damned impudence, I told him—he said Moon was a fascinating name—and perhaps that was why you'd married me.
DELIA (*smiling*) Did he? How sweet!
MOON. Sweet? What's sweet about it? (*He stares suspiciously at Delia*)
DELIA (*smilingly*) Yes, Henry?

(MOON *is about to say something, then checks himself*)

MOON. No—never mind.
DELIA (*rising and crossing to the sofa*) Did you have a nice lunch at the club? (*She sits on the sofa at the left end, removes her spectacles and puts them in her handbag*)
MOON. No, liver and bacon—worse than usual. But that's beside the point.
DELIA. I didn't know there was a point.
MOON. Certainly there's a point. A fellow says an idiotic thing like that over the phone—girl on the switch-board listening, probably—and all you can say is, "How sweet!" The same fellow has you to lunch—then goes to sleep—while you sit waiting here with your car outside.
DELIA. I could hardly bring it inside.
MOON (*angrily*) You know what I mean.
DELIA. No, I don't. Do you?
MOON (*crossing above the easy chair to* C; *impressively*) Delia.
DELIA. Yes, Henry?

MOON (*impressively*) I'm going to put two straight questions to you—and I want two straight truthful answers.
DELIA. Are you sure?
MOON. Sure? Of course I'm sure. Why shouldn't I be?
DELIA (*gently*) Because I've never felt you liked the truth, Henry.
MOON (*staggered*) My godfathers! *Me!* Not like the truth? What are you talking about? Let anybody show me the facts, and I'm always ready to face them. Ask them at the office. Ask them at the club. Why, some people think I overdo it. "You're too outspoken, Henry, old boy," some people say.
DELIA. Don't let's bother about those people, Henry. You just be outspoken. Two straight questions—two straight truthful answers. Go on.
MOON (*impressively*) Number one, then. Have I—or have I not—played the game with you, Delia?
DELIA. You've played *your* game with me, Henry—but not *my* game with me.
MOON. I don't know what that means—doubt if you do—but we'll leave it for the time being. The next question's more important. (*Very impressively*) Are you playing the game, Delia?
DELIA. Do you mean—am I being unfaithful to you, Henry?
MOON (*perturbed by such plain speech; hastily*) Certainly not. I'm not talking on those lines at all. I know what you want to do. You want me to say more than I mean—then you turn round and ask me what the devil I mean by accusing you of this, that and the other. Oh—no, I'm not having that. You don't catch me falling for that one, my dear girl. No fear! I'm just putting a simple straight question to you. Are you playing the game?
DELIA (*losing her temper*) But it isn't a simple straight question at all. It just doesn't mean anything. What game? If you mean—am I having an affair—why don't you say so?
MOON (*shouting*) Because I'm not going to be jockeyed into a false position and have you making a fool of me. It's an old trick—and this time it won't work.
DELIA (*raising her voice*) Then what on earth *are* you talking about?
MOON (*angrily*) Well, for instance, your car's out there, isn't it? Been out there for two or three hours. Nobody could miss it. As soon as I came round the corner, I knew you must be here. There must be other people who must be thinking the same thing. They'll start talking—probably doing it now. That's not good enough, is it? You can't call that playing the game—not in a town like this.
DELIA (*goading him*) You mean—they aren't playing the game when they start talking?
MOON (*goaded: loudly and wildly*) No, of course I don't—and you know dam' well I don't, Delia. I mean *you* aren't playing

the game when you give 'em an excuse to talk—or when you're just staying on here, when you don't know who might come in, instead of clearing out, or for that matter when you even have lunch with a fellow who's behaving so queerly and other fellows are already wondering about him. And I say I've played the game with you—and now you're not playing the game with me—that's all.

(KETTLE *enters from the bedroom. He looks pleasantly tousled and relaxed, and is lighting his pipe.* MOON *moves above the easy chair*)

KETTLE (*crossing to* C) Oh—hello—Moon.
MOON (*indignantly*) Hello, Kettle.
DELIA (*lovingly*) Did you have a nice sleep?
KETTLE (*smilingly*) Wonderful!
DELIA (*lovingly*) I hope we didn't wake you.
MOON (*indignantly*) And I must say this seems to me a bit much. Did he have a nice sleep? I hope we didn't wake him! Who is he, anyhow—the Shah of Persia? He ought to be doing his job at the London and North Midland Bank now—never mind his nice sleep. Now I'll put a straight question to you, Kettle . . .
DELIA (*to Kettle*) Henry's putting straight questions this afternoon.
MOON (*to Kettle*) What do you think you're up to?

(KETTLE, *comfortably smoking, looks from Moon to Delia, then back to Moon*)

KETTLE (*slowly*) Well, Moon, old chap . . .
MOON (*cutting in; indignantly*) Never mind about the "Moon, old chap"—we're not on those terms.
KETTLE. You prefer Mr Moon? I'm delighted. I like Mr Moon. Well, Mr Moon. I'm not up to anything at the moment, as you see. I'm just taking it easy—as you see, smoking—pure Latakia, too. I've always wanted to smoke pure Latakia.
DELIA. It has an enchanting smell.
KETTLE. It has, hasn't it? I never dared to smoke it before because it's supposed to be bad for one.
MOON. Bad for you?
KETTLE. That's why I'm smoking it now. And that's about all I'm up to at the moment, Mr Moon. What do you suggest?
MOON. I suggest you try what I've tried, Kettle. And what I've tried—is to play the game.
KETTLE (*interested*) I overheard you talking about that. Which game? You know, I bought a Jungle Shooting Game this morning . . .
MOON (*cutting in; loudly*) I'm talking about doing the Decent Thing.

(DELIA *laughs.* MOON *glares at her*)

C

DELIA. I'm sorry, Henry. You looked so funny, that's all.
MOON (*with dignity*) As soon as you're ready to listen properly, I'll carry on.
KETTLE. Delia, behave yourself.
DELIA (*meekly*) Yes, George.
MOON (*indignantly*) And I must say—it's a bit much when a fellow has to listen to another fellow telling his wife to behave herself . . .
KETTLE (*cutting in; gravely*) Quite right, Mr Moon. It *is* a bit much. But you were talking about doing the decent thing.
MOON. I expect other people to try and do what I've always tried to do, to play the game. What I have done, in spite of many temptations.
DELIA (*interested*) Really, Henry. And you never told me.
MOON. Naturally not. But you can take my word for it—they were there.
KETTLE (*with immense mock gravity*) Isn't that rather too vague, Mr Moon? Oughtn't you to give us a definite example?
DELIA. Of course he ought. Especially as this is the first I've heard of them.
KETTLE (*with immense mock gravity*) Remember—unless you can convince us on this point, your whole argument falls to the ground.
DELIA (*encouragingly*) Now, Henry. Who, for instance? (*She moves along the seat of the sofa to the right end*)
MOON (*crossing and sitting on the sofa at the left end; doubtfully*) All very well—but don't want to talk like a cad, y'know.
DELIA. I don't mind. I like cads' talk.
KETTLE (*moving to the easy chair and sitting*) And I *am* a cad from now on. So . . .?
MOON. Well—for example—there's a Miss Carson in our office—often acts as my assistant . . .
DELIA (*interested*) Is that the bulgy red-haired one?
MOON (*with dignity*) Miss Carson *has* auburn hair—and an unusually fine figure. She's—er—rather devoted to me. At least my partner Jack Francis always says so—pulls my leg about it.
KETTLE (*encouragingly*) Good! I pass Miss Carson as a temptation.
MOON. Well, several times Miss Carson and I have had to spend a night away from Brickmill—on important business. And what's happened?
DELIA (*enjoying this*) Yes, what *has* happened, Henry?
MOON (*with massive anti-climax*) Nothing.
KETTLE. Nothing?
MOON. Nothing. After a hard day's work together, I've stood her a spot of dinner and perhaps a few drinks afterwards, but we've been jolly good pals, that's all—just jolly good pals.
DELIA. I'll bet Miss Carson hates being a jolly good pal.

Act II   MR KETTLE AND MRS MOON

Moon. That's not the point. I appeal to you, Kettle.
Kettle. Quite right, Moon. Not the point. We're talking about you now, not Miss Carson. She's merely the temptation you've resisted.
Moon. Quite. The point is—I've stuck to my guns.
Kettle. A very happy way of putting it, too.
Moon. Delia and I may not have been getting along as well as we might—though I don't think we've made a bad show of it—but if she played the game with me, I was ready to play the game with her.
Kettle. If she stuck to her guns, you would stick to your guns.
Moon. Absolutely.
Delia (*impatiently*) I wish you'd stop sticking to your guns, Henry, and simply tell me what you think.
Moon. That's the point. What am I to think?
Kettle (*sympathetically*) Well, what would you like to think, Mr Moon?
Moon (*angrily*) It isn't a question of what I think but of what other people will think. Just remember that. (*He glances at his watch and rises*) I must go. (*He collects his hat and umbrella*)

(Kettle *rises, moves to the door* L *and opens it*)

Got an important appointment at four. Two fellows coming from London to look at the Murchison factory—fine property. Very big deal, if it comes off. (*He looks appealingly at them*) Let's try and keep our heads, shall we? There's a right and a wrong way even in this sort of thing. After all, none of us can afford a scandal, can we?
Kettle. Yes, I can. One of the few things I can afford, from now on.
Moon (*crossing to the door* L) If you'll take my tip, Kettle—you'll be careful—very, very careful. You're going too far along the line. You going home, Delia?
Delia. No, not yet, Henry.
Moon. Talk things over, eh? Quite right. Well, I must run.

(Moon *exits* L. Delia *and* Kettle *wait for a moment, looking meaningly at each other*)

Delia (*softly*) Well, that's Henry. You see what I meant?
Kettle (*crossing to the desk*) I do. What's the telephone number of his office?
Delia. Eight-three-five-seven. Why?
Kettle (*lifting the receiver*) I have an urgent message for Miss Carson. (*He dials and listens*) Number engaged. (*He holds the receiver and waits*)

(Delia *rises and moves above the sofa.*
Monica *enters from the kitchen*)

Delia. Hello—I thought you'd gone, Monica.

MONICA. Raining too hard. So I washed up. But I thought I'd tell you I get the idea now. I was a bit dumb, wasn't I? I'm going now but I'll be back. I want to know what happens—an' there might be something I can do. Boy, is my face red?

(MONICA *exits to the kitchen.* KETTLE, *still at the telephone, looks enquiringly at Delia*)

KETTLE. What's that about?

DELIA (*half-laughing*) She had designs on you.

KETTLE (*dialling*) Nonsense! She's only a kid.

DELIA. She's a full-grown female, complete with assorted designs.

KETTLE (*into the telephone*) Is that Moon and Francis? . . . I want to speak to Miss Carson, please . . . Yes, yes, very important . . . (*He waits*)

(DELIA *moves to the dining-table, collects the table mats, puts them in the table drawer and finds a revolver in the drawer, which she takes out*)

Miss Carson? . . . This is a friend—a well-wisher. Now don't you take any more of that "jolly good pal" nonsense from Henry Moon. That man's crazy about you . . . Yes, you ought to have seen the look in his eye when he described your figure. He's raving and drooling. All the best, Miss Carson. (*He replaces the receiver to break the call, then puts the receiver on the desk*)

DELIA (*showing him the revolver; seriously*) Why this thing?

KETTLE (*carelessly*) The Bank gave every manager one some time ago when the crime wave started. But it doesn't work very well and it's doubtful if I could hit anything with it.

DELIA. I could. My father taught me . . .

KETTLE (*cutting in*) Give it to me, my pet. (*He takes the revolver from Delia, puts it in the desk drawer, then leads Delia to the easy chair*) Let's talk about ourselves—or even Henry.

DELIA (*sitting in the easy chair*) I don't want to talk about Henry.

(KETTLE *sits on the right arm of the easy chair*)

You see, though, what I meant—about nothing being real.

KETTLE. I'm not sure you're very real yet. But better, not worse.

DELIA. That's the wrong way to talk, darling. I'm very real.

KETTLE. Of course. But we've allowed ourselves to be bullied out of any genuine belief in happiness. So we think it can't be real.

DELIA. That's men, not women.

KETTLE. Then women should never have let it happen to men. They ought to have stopped it. (*He looks smilingly at her*) When do we go, Delia? Tonight?

DELIA (*looking steadily at him*) Go? Where?

KETTLE. I don't know. Anywhere. Just go.
DELIA. But, darling, why should we go?
KETTLE (*astonished*) But—but—you don't imagine I'm staying on here, do you? I thought it was obvious from the first I was clearing out.
DELIA. This morning—yes.
KETTLE. Well—what's happened since . . .?
DELIA (*cutting in; smilingly*) Me. Us.
KETTLE (*rising and moving* C) You. Us. Certainly—but I tell you, I've finished with the bank—and with this town and any town that looks like this—with all this sort of life.
DELIA. But what does it matter *now*? I know how you felt—I felt it, too—but now we can laugh at it together—so everything's different.
KETTLE. Not for me it isn't.
DELIA. In other words, loving me isn't enough for you—though loving you would be enough for me?
KETTLE. That's not a fair question.
DELIA (*impatiently*) Oh—don't be like Henry.
KETTLE. That's just what I'm trying not to be—like Henry. What are you asking me to do—pretend all day long?
DELIA. Women have to do it—all day long and half the night.
KETTLE. I thought you didn't want to be that sort of woman.
DELIA (*rising*) I didn't say I did. But I'm trying to be sensible for both of us.
KETTLE (*crossing below the sofa to* R; *rather heatedly*) Don't bother about me. I've stopped being sensible.
DELIA (*not taking his tone; pleading*) That was all right this morning. And I loved you for it. But one of us *has* to be sensible. You talk about going—but you don't know where you want to go—or what you want to do when you get there.
KETTLE (*crossing above the sofa to* C; *heatedly*) That doesn't matter at this moment.
DELIA (*moving to* L *of Kettle; sharply*) Of course it does. We're not children. Nobody's going to look after us.
KETTLE (*urgently*) I tell you, Delia, all that matters is this. Do we go together—or do I go alone? (*Firmly*) Because I'm not staying here. I've done with it all.
DELIA (*hotly*) Which means that I haven't enough to keep you here.
KETTLE (*hotly*) I never thought for a moment you'd want to stay.
DELIA. And what do we do if we don't? Try for a job as cook and barman at a third-rate hotel?
KETTLE (*heatedly*) I'd rather be a barman in a fifth-rate hotel than a Brickmill bank manager enjoying another man's wife. I'd feel a rat and very soon I'd *be* a rat. Delia, this isn't really you. It's putting those dam' clothes on again that's done it.

DELIA (*crossing below Kettle to the arch up* R; *furiously*) You needn't remind me that I took them off for you.
KETTLE (*angrily*) Well—there are some I've taken off for ever—black coat, striped trousers, stiff collar.
DELIA (*turning to him; angrily*) I suppose I'm not even worth a stiff collar now.

(*There is a ringing and knocking at the front door off*)

Oh—damn! Now there's somebody here. (*She stands above the right end of the sofa*)
KETTLE. We ought to have locked that door again. (*He moves towards the door* L)

(*There is a sharp rap on the door* L.
STREET *and* HARDACRE *enter* L)

STREET (*closing the door; heartily*) Back again, you see, like I promised.
KETTLE (*crossing to* C) Go away.
HARDACRE (*moving* LC; *pointedly*) I think we passed your husband in his car, Mrs Moon.
DELIA. He's just been here, so don't bother throwing him at me.
KETTLE. In fact, don't bother about anything, Alderman Hardacre. Just go away.
STREET. Now—now—now, Mr Kettle.
HARDACRE (*angrily*) I'm not going away until I've said what I've come to say. There's nobody at that bank of yours understands about my Extension Loan.
KETTLE (*with obvious controlled fury*) I'm in the middle of the most important, the most urgent argument I ever had in my life—(*letting go*) and you have to come blundering in, blathering about your Extension Loan. *Go away!*
HARDACRE (*loudly and angrily*) You may think you're smart, Kettle, but I know it was you that rang me up this morning telling me life's wonderful. Well, now I'll tell you something, Kettle. I got on to your district Head Office this morning, and the chief inspector, Mr Clinton, has come to Brickmill specially—to talk to you. Now make something wonderful out of *that*.
STREET. It's quite true. I came to tell you . . .
HARDACRE (*triumphantly*) But seeing as I'd fixed it for him to come over, I thought I'd have the satisfaction of telling you myself.

(KETTLE *ignores Street and Hardacre and crosses to* L *of Delia*)

KETTLE (*to Delia*) Now—do you see what you're asking me to do?
DELIA. What does it matter about *them*? The point is, I asked you to do something for *me*.

KETTLE. It isn't for you—not as I see you.
DELIA. Perhaps you aren't seeing me.
HARDACRE (*angrily*) What he will be seeing soon is Mr Clinton, his boss. And Mr Clinton'll be asking him what he's playing at.
DELIA (*crossly*) Oh—shut up about your Mr Clinton.
HARDACRE (*nastily*) I'd like to know where you come into it. I must say, if I was Henry Moon . . .
KETTLE (*crossing to* C; *threatening Hardacre*) *Go away!*
HARDACRE. I *am* going. (*He moves quickly* L *and turns*) But you haven't finished with me yet.
DELIA (*in disgust*) Oh—surely!
HARDACRE. I'll see you later, Superintendent.

(HARDACRE *exits* L, *slamming the door behind him.* STREET *shakes his head, makes a tutting sound, then sits in the easy chair*)

STREET (*cheerfully*) He's a bit short-tempered and hasty, Alderman Hardacre is. But don't you worry about him, Mrs Moon. And don't worry about *me*. You get on with your argument.
KETTLE (*beginning with controlled fury*) As you noticed this morning, Superintendent, I've become rather eccentric. And one form it takes is this—strange as it may seem, I don't seem to know how to conduct an intimate argument with a woman—(*letting go now; furiously*) if a police superintendent's listening to us.
STREET. Sorry about that, Mr Kettle. You see, I arranged to meet Mr Clinton here.
DELIA (*moving to* R *of Kettle; smoothly*) George, how well do you know Superintendent Street?
KETTLE. Not very well. Why?
DELIA (*crossing below Kettle to the window and picking up her housecoat*) He's far more artful and dangerous than he seems to be. That's all. So be careful.
STREET. Be careful about what?
DELIA (*moving to Kettle; ignoring Street*) He seems stupid. But he isn't. And I don't like that sly cat-with-a-mouse tone of his. So watch him. (*She crosses to the arch up* R)
STREET (*slyly*) That's not the way out, Mrs Moon.
DELIA (*sweetly*) I'm going to the bathroom—do you mind?

(DELIA *exits up* R, *taking the housecoat with her.* KETTLE *looks after her then glares at* STREET, *who smiles broadly at him. During the ensuing scene,* KETTLE *paces irritably up and down*)

STREET. Wonderful how the ladies soon make themselves at home, isn't it?
KETTLE. Couldn't you go and mind your own business?
STREET. Well, strictly speaking, you can't say anything isn't our business. There are so many ways of breaking the law now.
KETTLE. Too many ways, too many laws.

STREET (*heartily*) Well, you're all right, Mr Kettle. Kept your promise I think, didn't you? Stayed in, eh?
KETTLE (*abruptly*) Yes.
STREET. Not been lonely, I fancy.
KETTLE (*abruptly*) I'm not lonely now. Thanks for calling. Good-bye.
STREET. We learn a lot in police work. Full of human nature, it is.
KETTLE. Very interesting. But some other time.
STREET (*expansively*) I've noticed many a time the way some ladies, often seemingly the quietest, are attracted to a man the minute he goes a bit wild or a bit cracked. It doesn't last, of course—they've too much sense—but they can't help being fascinated.
KETTLE. You must have a lot of time to waste.
STREET. When a man gets to my position in police work, Mr Kettle, he doesn't charge in when the harm's done but does a bit of intelligent anticipation. Have you ever noticed how little trouble we have here in Brickmill?
KETTLE. I used to live near that big cemetery at Hendon. They'd very little trouble there, too.
STREET. Now, now, Mr Kettle. Let me make my point. Intelligent anticipation. Of course you've done nothing illegal—that we know of—but when a good steady man suddenly goes off the rails, I can't help being interested in him.
KETTLE. Before the pattern was quite fixed, they were probably talking like that in ant hills.
STREET (*shaking his head*) That's far-fetched, Mr Kettle.
KETTLE. I'm all for the far-fetched, Superintendent. From now on I want to be a fanciful unsound man.
STREET. You wouldn't if you'd seen what I've seen. I've helped to put dozens of 'em behind bars.

(*The front door bell rings off*)

That might be your chief—Mr Clinton.
KETTLE (*moving to the door* L) Well, this time I'll see for myself who it is. So you stay there.

(STREET *rises*.
KETTLE *exits* L.
MR CLINTON *and* KETTLE *enter* L. CLINTON *is a well-dressed man about sixty, with an easy fatherly manner, a dangerous type*)

CLINTON (*moving* LC) Ah—Superintendent, we meet again.
STREET. We do, Mr Clinton. And what about your medical friend?

(KETTLE *crosses to* RC)

CLINTON. He'll be at our disposal in about a quarter of an hour or so.

KETTLE. What are you proposing to do—take my temperature?
CLINTON (*crossing to* L *of Kettle*) Just whatever you'd like us to do, Mr Kettle. I'm here as your colleague. I work for the London and North Midland too. No doubt our friend Hardacre thinks I'm now shouting at you, threatening you with this and that. All right—let him think so. But the truth is, it's you I care about —not him. A good manager's more important to us than a good account. You see, I'm perfectly frank with you, Kettle.
STREET. And, if I may say so, it's a pleasure to listen to you, Mr Clinton.
KETTLE (*moving down* R) It must be. And I'll tell you why. He's in your line of business, only further along and higher up.

(DELIA *enters from the bedroom. She wears her hat and is obviously ready to leave*)

CLINTON (*moving above the table* L *of the sofa; rather surprised*) Oh—good afternoon—Mrs Kettle.
DELIA (*dryly*) I'm not Mrs Kettle.
KETTLE (*moving to* L *of Clinton; hastily*) Mr Clinton—Mrs Moon.
CLINTON. How d'you do?
DELIA. How d'you do? (*She glances at Kettle*) I must go in a minute.
KETTLE. Mr. Clinton's your spokesman. You'd better stay and listen to what he says, and what I have to say to him. Any objections, Mr Clinton?
CLINTON (*hesitating*) It's—er—rather irregular . . .
DELIA. Oh—if it's irregular, I'll stay and listen. But, George, please, don't be childish.
STREET. Quite right, Mrs Moon.
DELIA. Don't *you* tell me that. You make me feel I must be wrong.
KETTLE. You *are* wrong. (*He indicates the easy chair* LC)

(CLINTON *crosses to the easy chair and sits.* DELIA *stands above the right end of the sofa*)

(*He moves* C) Well, Mr Clinton?
CLINTON. You've had a long training at the bank, long experience. You're known to be an excellent branch manager, the kind of man who would soon be promoted to a bigger branch.
DELIA (*in dismay; involuntarily*) Oh—no!
CLINTON. I beg your pardon?
DELIA (*moving below the sofa and sitting*) No, go on.

(KETTLE *sits on the left arm of the sofa.* STREET *stands down* L)

CLINTON. You're valuable to us, Kettle. We need you, my dear fellow. It's as simple as that.

KETTLE. Let's suppose it is. The bank needs me, but do I need the bank?
CLINTON. I'll come to that. You've taken a day off. All right. Take a week off. Take a month, if you give us a doctor's certificate. Only regard the bank as your friend.
KETTLE. But I don't want it as my friend. I've had enough of it.
CLINTON. What you do want is a break. You've gone stale.
KETTLE. I'm stale, so I have a break to freshen myself up. To become stale again. Perhaps to become stale for ever, sitting at the bottom of the Dead Sea. Or do I exaggerate, Mrs Moon?
DELIA. No, you just turn poetical at the wrong time, Mr Kettle.
CLINTON (*rising and moving* C) You've been with us over twenty years. Why throw them away for a mood?
KETTLE. Why throw the rest of my life away for a bank?
CLINTON. You have to earn a living?
KETTLE. Certainly. I've only saved a few hundreds.
CLINTON. What do you propose to do then?
KETTLE. I've no idea. (*He looks at Delia*) Something fairly disreputable—with irregular hours.
CLINTON. We guarantee you enviable security, my dear Kettle —what everybody wants.
KETTLE. Perhaps they're wrong to want it.
STREET. Well, half the crimes are committed looking for it.
KETTLE. Perhaps *all* the crimes are committed looking for it. Perhaps that's where we've all gone wrong.
CLINTON. Very few people would agree with you.
KETTLE (*rising and moving above the sofa*) That's the kind of man I want to be——

(CLINTON *moves up* L)

—that very few people agree with. I've spent years and years agreeing with everybody.
STREET (*heavily*) Security's well worth having. It stands to reason.
KETTLE. Well, it can stop standing to reason. I've had my share of security. Now I'll take insecurity. Up one week, down the next. Tea and stale bread this Tuesday. Champagne and smoked salmon next Tuesday.
STREET. That's boys' talk.
KETTLE (*moving* C) Well, didn't you like being a boy?
STREET. Yes, but I had to grow up—to think and behave like a man.
KETTLE. Does that include taking the boy in you and wringing his neck?
STREET. It might have to.
KETTLE. Last week I didn't even feel I was a man. Today I do. A boy *and* a man—better still.

CLINTON (*moving* LC) A conscientious boy? A responsible man? We have to keep the world going, you know, Kettle.
KETTLE. The world we enjoy, certainly. But there are different worlds.
CLINTON. There's only one that keeps *us* going.
KETTLE. I doubt it. But I know what you want to say. "What would happen . . .?" Go on . . .
CLINTON. Very well. What would happen if every man walked away from his work as you did this morning?
KETTLE. How did you come here this morning?
CLINTON. I caught the twelve forty-five from Birmingham. Why?
KETTLE. What would have happened if everybody in Birmingham had tried to catch the twelve forty-five?
CLINTON (*protesting*) Now, wait a minute . . .
STREET (*cutting in; puzzled*) There's a catch there somewhere.
DELIA. I wonder if there is.
KETTLE (*turning to Delia*) Not as big a catch, Delia, as there's been in that "What would happen if everybody did it?" line of argument. It's been one of the great flatteners, bleachers and dimmers of life. To hell with what would happen if everybody did it! Why not assume people are different? Even now some of 'em are.
CLINTON. But if the whole staff of our branch here had walked out as you did . . .
KETTLE (*cutting in*) Why suppose anything of the kind? Young Morgan, for instance, is as anxious to be a bank manager as I am to stop being one. All right, let him. He goes in. I go out.
CLINTON. But why—Kettle—why?
KETTLE. Because I've had enough.
DELIA (*jumping up*) And so have I.
KETTLE (*turning to her: alarmed*) Delia!
DELIA. No. Not enough of you. But I want to think. Look! (*She moves with deliberation to the telephone, replaces the receiver then turns to Kettle*) Don't take this off again. I'll ring you up.
KETTLE. To say what?
DELIA. I don't know yet. I tell you, I want to think. And I don't know what I'm thinking with you three men shouting at one another. (*She looks at the other two*) You won't persuade him, you know. I see that now. Well, you won't succeed where I failed, that's one consolation.
KETTLE. Delia!
DELIA. No, George, don't let's say any more now.

(DELIA *crosses and exits hurriedly* L. KETTLE *makes a move to follow her, but the front door is heard to slam, before he can leave the room. He moves rather slowly and sombrely to the cabinet down* L)

KETTLE. Anybody want a drink?

CLINTON (*crossing and sitting on the sofa at the right end; rather primly*) Not at this time of day, thank you.

(KETTLE *pours a whisky and soda for himself*)

STREET (*moving L of the easy chair*) Same here. And if you'll take my tip, Mr Kettle——

KETTLE (*cutting in; neatly but not rudely*) I'm not taking your tip, Superintendent. (*He crosses to* C) I've no intention of turning into a drunk, but from now on when I feel like having a drink I'm going to have one. (*He raises his glass*) Your health, gentlemen! God rest you—may nothing you dismay. (*He drinks. Slowly and reflectively*) Y'know, I believe one of two things happens to men of my age who aren't really living. Either they die inside—and Brickmill's full of men who died years ago—or they live in a fashion by turning into haters of a full warm existence, into large grey rats just gnawing away at the good life.

CLINTON (*dryly*) Which are we, by the way, walking dead men or large grey rats?

KETTLE (*mildly thoughtful*) I think you're rats. Enemies of what I take to be the good life.

CLINTON. And what's that?

KETTLE. I can't define it. If I could, I'd be able to see all round it, which would mean it would be smaller than I am. Therefore, not the good life.

STREET (*rather roughly*) Your good life's going to be a nervous breakdown. Already you're irresponsible.

KETTLE. Certainly. From now on, gentlemen, I propose to dodge by every possible means all the responsibilities and commitments of the decent sound British citizen—poor devil!

CLINTON (*dryly*) Do you indeed?

KETTLE (*expanding*) I do. Money previously spent on taxes, rates, insurance premiums, subscriptions, will now be spent on constant travel, food and drink, gorgeous clothes for the woman I'm living with, and occasional evenings with symphony orchestras. I shall hobnob almost entirely with cheerful riff-raff, be polite only to nice pleasant people, and be downright rude to bigwigs, stuffed shirts and pompous busybodies. (*He moves to the desk and puts his drink on it*) And now, gentlemen, no more argument. You can have a drink, play a shooting game or the drum and cymbals with me—or go away.

STREET. See what I mean, Mr Clinton? Everything topsy-turvy.

CLINTON (*rising*) Our friend's probably outside now, waiting for one of us.

KETTLE (*moving to L of the dining-table*) If you mean your medical friend, you're wasting his time. I haven't felt better for years. (*He lights his pipe*)

STREET (*with sinister intonation*) Sometimes a doctor's certificate will excuse something that otherwise might get a man into serious trouble.

(*During the dialogue leading to the knock-out,* CLINTON *and* STREET *advance slowly towards Kettle*)

CLINTON (*with sinister intonation*) The Bank isn't very happy about branch managers who suddenly walk out and begin expressing extremely subversive sentiments. We wonder what's behind it all.

KETTLE (*dreamily*) I was quite right. Large grey rats.

CLINTON. Your accounts may be in order, Kettle, and then again they may not. Some men need more money than they're entitled to—to spend on travel, food and drink.

STREET (*tapping Kettle on the shoulder; nastily*) Or clothes for another man's wife. I noticed she took a dress in there that never came out—new and very saucy.

KETTLE (*losing his temper*) Oh—shut up—you damned lout! (*He tries to hit Street*)

(STREET *counters Kettle's blow then knocks him clean out, so that* KETTLE *falls unconscious to the floor,* L *of the easy chair*)

STREET (*standing over Kettle; coolly*) Thought he'd have a go at me for that last little packet I handed him. Worked out nicely, didn't it? You're a witness. I had to hit him in self-defence, didn't I, Mr Clinton?

CLINTON. You did. If Dr Grenock could do anything with him now . . .

STREET. That's what I had in mind, of course. Might be just right. You bring him in, while I keep an eye on our friend here.

CLINTON. Excellent.

(CLINTON *crosses and exits* L. STREET *bends over Kettle, making sure he is out.*

MONICA *enters hurriedly from the kitchen*)

MONICA (*as she enters*) I say, Mr Kettle . . . (*She breaks off*) Here, what's going on?

STREET (*angrily*) You keep out of this.

MONICA (*moving* C; *angrily*) I believe you knocked him out.

STREET (*angrily*) Self-defence. Go on. Pop off, girl.

(*The telephone rings.* STREET *moves to the telephone and lifts the receiver*)

(*Into the telephone*) Yes? . . . Oh—it's you, is it, Mrs Moon? Superintendent Street here . . . No, I can't give you Mr Kettle . . . He's out . . .

(MONICA *moves to Street, snatches the receiver from him and struggles with him to retain it*)

MONICA (*shouting into the telephone*) He's not out. He's knocked out. He's unconscious . . .

(STREET *recovers the receiver and pushes Monica down* C. MONICA *moves below the sofa.* STREET *replaces the receiver, then moves to Monica and puts a heavy hand on her shoulder*)

STREET (*angrily*) What's your name?

MONICA. Monica Twigg.

STREET (*angrily*) Well, Monica Twigg, you've obstructed a police officer in the course of his duty—and now you're under arrest.

MONICA (*excitedly*) Shall I have my photo in the paper?

STREET. You might.

MONICA (*delighted*) Oh—goody, goody, goody!

MONICA *sits happily on the sofa and grins at the glaring* STREET *as*—

the CURTAIN *falls*

ACT III

SCENE *The same. Early evening.*

When the CURTAIN *rises, it is about five minutes later.* STREET *is pacing up and down behind the sofa.* KETTLE, *still unconscious, is lying on the floor.* MONICA *is sitting on the sofa, at the right end.*

STREET (*with mock severity*) How d'you like scrubbing floors?
MONICA. I don't.
STREET. Well, that's what you'll be doing soon.
MONICA. Who says so?
STREET (*exasperated*) I say so. The magistrate'll say so. The matron of the Home'll say so. The warden'll say so.
MONICA. What about the Army an' Navy?

(DR GRENOCK *and* CLINTON *enter* L. *The* DOCTOR *is a formally-dressed, portentous man in his forties. He is not carrying the usual doctor's bag.* STREET *meets Clinton and the doctor* LC. MONICA *rises and moves up* R *of the easy chair*)

CLINTON (*introducing*) Superintendent Street—Dr Grenock.
DOCTOR. How d'you do? Excuse me for a moment. (*He makes a brief examination of the unconscious Kettle and is obviously satisfied by what he has observed*) Seems in good physical condition—fortunately. (*He is about to continue when he notices Monica*) Who's this?
STREET. Don't bother about her, Doctor. Under arrest for trying to obstruct a police officer.
MONICA (*complacently*) It'll say in the paper, "Pretty Girl Fights Police". (*She crosses and stands below the sofa*)
STREET. You be quiet. Is he all right for you like this, Doctor?
DOCTOR. If I treat him just when he's coming round. I understand he wouldn't have agreed to have hypnosis?
STREET. He'd never have allowed you to come near him. He's a rebel now—see?
MONICA. Good luck to him!
DOCTOR. It's not uncommon. A secondary suppressed self suddenly takes charge. A minor form of dissociated personality. Not major, otherwise the primary self wouldn't have functioned so efficiently. It would have been inadequate for his complete social integration. You wouldn't say he was inadequate, would you?
STREET. No. Good quiet steady citizen—well thought of—gave no trouble.
CLINTON. Excellent in his work for us.

DOCTOR. Quite so. Did he tell you what happened to him this morning?

STREET. Yes. He heard a voice asking him what it was all for.

MONICA (*complacently*) I've heard that voice—and there's no answer, neither.

STREET (*shouting*) What you'll hear in a minute, if you don't keep quiet, is a loud slapping noise.

(*The* DOCTOR *ignores the interruption and crosses above Street to* C)

DOCTOR. A voice—eh? Yes—yes—yes—the usual thing. Well, if I catch him just when he's coming round, a little quick neat hypnosis will do all that's necessary. I can restore the control of the primary self, which will at once suppress, probably to a fairly deep level, the rebellious secondary self.

(MONICA *edges to* R *of the Doctor*)

I can persuade him he's had some accident.

MONICA. So can I.

DOCTOR. Sh!

(MONICA *moves below the sofa*)

An interesting case. As the strain of modern life increases, with some inevitable loss of instinctive satisfactions . . . Let's put him on his bed, shall we? (*He motions to Street*)

(STREET *moves to Kettle and lifts him by the feet*)

(*He moves to Kettle and lifts him by the shoulders*) I say——

(STREET *and the* DOCTOR *move slowly towards the arch up* R)

—with some inevitable loss of instinctive satisfactions, and a growing sense of frustration on the unconscious level, there are bound to be more and more of these partial dissociations. And if we find we can cure them by light hypnosis, following some shock like this, then we've achieved a method of treatment that might be generally followed.

(*The* DOCTOR *and* STREET *exit with* KETTLE *to the bedroom.* MONICA *watches them go, then sits on the sofa at the right end.* CLINTON *moves to the desk, consults the telephone directory-pad, lifts the receiver, dials a number.*

MRS TWIGG *enters hurriedly from the kitchen and is astonished to see Monica*)

MRS TWIGG. Monica, what are you doin' 'ere?

CLINTON (*to Mrs Twigg*) Just a minute, please.

MRS TWIGG. Oo—I'm sorry.

CLINTON (*into the telephone*) Enquiries? . . . When's your next train to Birmingham? . . . No, that's too soon. What's the next? . . . Thank you. (*He replaces the receiver and moves to* R *of the easy chair*)

MRS TWIGG (*crossing to* C) I *do* beg your pardon, sir, but this is my daughter—and I can't think what she's doin' 'ere.
MONICA (*complacently*) I'm under arrest.
MRS TWIGG (*staggered*) Under arrest? My goodness me! Whatever have you done this time?
MONICA. How do you mean "this time"? I've never been arrested before.
MRS TWIGG. I should think not indeed.
MONICA. I might have my photo in the paper.
MRS TWIGG (*appalled*) An' then what will your Aunt Florrie say? We'll never hear the last of it. (*She turns to Clinton*) I never know whether she's tellin' the truth, these days. What's happened, sir?
CLINTON. Superintendent Street will be out in a minute. I don't think it's very serious.
MRS TWIGG. But where's Mr Kettle?
CLINTON. In his bedroom. The doctor's with him now.
MRS TWIGG (*triumphantly*) What did I tell you, Monica Twigg? Right from the first, didn't I say he was poorly?
MONICA. Go on. That Superintendent knocked him out. And now they're giving him what's-it—hypnotism—like I've seen at the pictures.
MRS TWIGG (*indignantly*) Now stop it, Monica. An' if you wasn't always going to the pictures an' readin' them picture papers, you wouldn't get such ideas. An' when it isn't pictures—it's all sex—sex—sex.
CLINTON (*moving* L) Quite true.
MONICA. Go on! You talk as if we'd invented it. Been going on a long time, hasn't it?
MRS TWIGG. Not on your scale, it hasn't. You think people have nothing else to do. Look what you said about poor Mr Kettle, when I told you he's not interested in sex—just doesn't fancy it.
MONICA. If you'd seen that posh glamorous housecoat that woman must have put on for him, and the look in her eye, like a cat full of cream, you would'nt say he didn't fancy it.
MRS TWIGG (*angrily*) I tell you it's out of all reason. A nasty Monday morning, too—when *nobody* fancies it.

(STREET *enters from the bedroom*)

STREET. When nobody fancies what?
MONICA (*promptly*) Sex.
STREET (*moving above the sofa; disapprovingly*) Well, now we *are* talking, aren't we? Haven't left school five minutes—and sitting there, bold as brass, talking about sex.
MONICA. I left school three years since.
MRS TWIGG. Don't take any notice of her, Superintendent. She doesn't know what she's saying half the time.

Monica. Yes, I do. She only gets mad at me because I can't keep a job long.

Street. And why can't you keep a job long?

Mrs Twigg (*innocently*)   Sex.

Street (*indignantly*)   Are *you* starting now?

Mrs Twigg. I only came to see if Mr Kettle might want a bit of something to eat. I could make him a nice shape an' a drop of custard.

Monica. An' serve him right if he stays here.

Street (*moving to* R *of Mrs Twigg*)   Call later, Mrs Twigg. (*He passes Mrs Twigg in front of him towards the kitchen door*) You're in the way now. And take that daughter of yours with you.

Monica (*rising; disappointed*)   D'you mean I'm not under arrest?

Street. Not this time.

Monica (*disgusted*)   Why—you don't know your own mind two minutes together.

Street (*roaring*)   *Outside!*

(Mrs Twigg *hastily pulls* Monica *off to the kitchen*)

(*Moving up* RC; *confidentially*)   I left the doctor to get on with it. Smart chap, I'd say.

Clinton (*crossing to* L *of Street*)   Very. I've used him before. We get nervous breakdowns now and again.

Street. I have an idea he'll pull it off.

Clinton. Then I'll be very grateful for the help you've given us, Superintendent.

Street. Don't mention it, Mr Clinton. Been a pleasure.

Clinton. But I'll tell you frankly I don't quite understand your interest in the case. Not really quite in your line of duty, surely?

Street. No. But when I left him here this morning—all free and easy, having actually enjoyed playing a kid's game with him, and him not caring tuppence—the thought of him suddenly put my back up. I'd got to get back to my work. And he ought to get back to his. Why, where would we all be if . . .?

Clinton (*cutting in; smoothly*)   Quite so. Exactly my own argument.

Street (*indignantly*)   And then you're called a large grey rat.

(*The telephone rings*)

(*He lifts the receiver. Into the telephone*) Yes? . . . Oh, Alderman Hardacre, this is Superintendent Street here . . . No, we think it's all under control . . . Yes, Mr Clinton's still here . . . Well, come round and see for yourself. (*He replaces the receiver*) Alderman Hardacre's hopping mad. Something about the Press . . .

Clinton (*cutting in; hastily*)   We don't want the Press brought into this.

STREET. That's what I thought. Well, you'll have to calm him down, Mr Clinton. He'll be here soon.

(*The front door bell rings off*)·

No, that can't be him. Even Hardacre couldn't be that quick. (*He moves* L)

(*There is a tap on the door* L)

(*He calls*) Come in.

(MOON *enters* L)

(*He moves to* R *of Moon*) Oh—hello, Mr Moon.

MOON. How are you, Superintendent?

STREET. Nicely. This is Mr Henry Moon—one of our leading estate agents. Mr Clinton—district head of the London and North Midland Bank.

MOON (*crossing to Clinton and shaking hands with him*) Great pleasure, Mr Clinton. Come to take charge? Quite right, quite right. (*He hesitates a moment*) By the way, my wife's not here, is she?

STREET (*moving to* L *of Moon*) She *was* here, then went. But then we had a telephone call from her, and it's my belief she's now on her way back. So if you want to see her, you'd better wait.

MOON. Very well. But what about Kettle?

STREET. He's here.

MOON (*solemnly*) I've a bone to pick with him.

STREET. You'll have to wait. (*He indicates the bedroom*) Doctor's picking a bone with him just now. But I don't think he'll be long.

MOON. Kettle's a sick man, is he?

STREET. In a manner of speaking.

CLINTON (*gravely*) Some temporary nervous trouble, Mr Moon.

MOON (*portentously*) You don't surprise me, you don't surprise me at all. I was here earlier, and I said to myself then, "Henry, old boy, keep your temper," I said, "you're dealing with a sick man—unbalanced," I said. Kept phoning my office—all kinds of dam' nonsense. Quite upset my assistant, Miss Carson. (*To Clinton. Earnestly*) How d'you find business conditions, Mr Clinton?

CLINTON (*solemnly*) Favourable on the whole, Mr Moon—very favourable.

MOON. Glad to hear you say so, Mr Clinton. Same trend here. Things are moving nicely in Brickmill. Just negotiated an option on the old Murchison factory—you know it, Superintendent . . .

STREET (*heartily*) Know it well.

MOON (*complacently*) Looks like being a very big deal—six figures. Between ourselves, of course.

D*

STREET (*confidentially*) Yes—and while we're talking between ourselves—Mr Moon—I think if I were you, I wouldn't let Mrs Moon stay here very long.

CLINTON. I quite agree, Mr Moon.

MOON (*looking from one to the other*) Oh, you do, do you? Take a firm line there, you think?

STREET (*confidentially*) That's my advice—unofficially, of course, as a friend. Just put your foot down, Mr Moon.

MOON. Shouldn't be necessary. Just a quiet word ought to do it. But—er—any particular reason?

CLINTON (*tactfully*) It's a delicate situation here—you know, Mr Moon—men's business.

MOON. Quite, quite. (*He crosses to R of the sofa*) See what you mean.

STREET (*confidentially*) As soon as women come into the picture, you never quite know where you are, do you?

MOON. Never. Noticed it many a time.

CLINTON. I've sometimes had a notion that in a properly planned world, you'd have to set them apart somehow, where they couldn't make mischief, except among themselves.

MOON. It's a thought, old man. Very well—I'll just . . .

(*But we never learn what he will do because at that moment the door L bursts open.*

DELIA *enters* L. *She is dressed in travelling clothes, but looks much less severe than she did originally. She is a fierce creature now, full of fire and determination*)

DELIA. Where is he?

STREET. In the bedroom. A doctor's with him.

DELIA. You hurt him.

CLINTON (*hastily*) No, don't worry.

STREET. He's all right.

DELIA (*crossing quickly to the arch up R*) I'll go and see.

(DELIA *darts into the bedroom*)

MOON (*rushing to the arch up R and calling*) Delia! Delia!

(*The three men stare after Delia, not knowing what to do. After a moment vague sounds are heard from the bedroom, of* DELIA's *voice and the* DOCTOR's *voice raised in expostulation. Then the* DOCTOR's *voice can be heard quite clearly*)

DOCTOR (*off; calling urgently*) Superintendent! Superintendent!

(*The* DOCTOR *rushes on from the bedroom*)

STREET (*crossing to the arch up R*) I'm here.

(*The* DOCTOR *and* STREET *exit to the bedroom. A scuffling sound is heard off*)

ACT III   MR KETTLE AND MRS MOON   49

(*Off*) Now you just be sensible, Mrs Moon.

(STREET *and the* DOCTOR, *with* DELIA *between them, struggling a little, enter from the bedroom.* CLINTON *moves to the easy chair*)

DOCTOR (*indignantly*) I assure you, madam, that I can't possibly allow you to disturb us like that. I speak for the patient as well as for myself. If you'll just wait, you'll be able to see for yourself what my treatment has done for him. But we can't possibly be interrupted now. Otherwise I couldn't guarantee anything. Superintendent, please make sure we're not disturbed again.

STREET. Certainly.

(*The* DOCTOR *exits to the bedroom*)

(*He releases Delia*) Now, Mrs Moon . . .

(DELIA *glares at Street, then moves away, ignoring Clinton and Moon*)

(*He looks significantly at Moon*) Mr Moon?

MOON (*crossing to* R *of Delia; not happy about this*) Yes, of course, old man. (*Hesitantly*) Delia. You ought to go home.

DELIA (*impatiently*) Who says so?

MOON (*uncertainly*) Well—I do.

DELIA (*dismissing him*) Don't be silly, Henry.

MOON (*rather bolder now*) And *they* do, too.

DELIA (*more interested now*) You mean—these two?

MOON. Delicate situation here. Men's business, old girl.

DELIA. Please be quiet, Henry.

(MOON *retires to* R *of the sofa*)

(*She looks hard at the other two*) Now tell me what happened. And no lies, please.

STREET. I don't tell lies, Mrs Moon.

DELIA. You do. You told me he'd gone out.

STREET. Not *gone* out. I said he *was* out. I'd had to knock him out.

DELIA. Why?

STREET. Because he attacked me.

DELIA. Why did he attack you?

STREET. Didn't like something I said, I suppose.

CLINTON (*with authority*) My dear Mrs Moon, you must realize that Kettle had been mentally unbalanced all day . . .

STREET. Even called us horrible names.

DELIA. What names?

STREET. He said we were large grey rats.

MOON. Good Lord! I must say . . .

DELIA. Don't say anything, Henry. Leave this to me. (*To the other two*) Perhaps you were behaving like large grey rats. I wouldn't put it past you. Where was this doctor when all this happened? Where does he come in?

CLINTON. He's a specialist we employ. It happened we had an appointment . . .

DELIA. Here?

CLINTON. Yes.

DELIA. To do what?

CLINTON. Really, I can't see that's any concern of yours. I'm here on bank business.

DELIA. And I'm here on personal business—much more important.

STREET. You just remember you've no reason to be here that would sound well in a court of law.

DELIA. For that matter, neither have you. You've been dodging in and out all day as if this was a police station and not a man's house. Did he ask you to come here and knock him out?

STREET (*crossing down* L *of the easy chair; angrily*) Mr Moon, if you can't make her go, at least make her keep quiet.

MOON (*sitting on the sofa at the right end*) Easier said than done, old man.

DELIA (*grimly enumerating her points*) Calls you rats—unbalanced—gets knocked out—(*she moves* C) specialist on the spot—the thumping lie you told me on the telephone—this fishy committee of welcome—and you want me to clear out. Pooh! There isn't a woman on earth who'd be satisfied with this situation. What's that doctor supposed to be doing in there?

CLINTON. Giving Kettle some necessary treatment.

DELIA. Treatment for *what*?

CLINTON. We're all living under a considerable strain these days.

DELIA. Are we? Why?

CLINTON (*testily*) Because, my dear madam, we can't help it.

DELIA. Why? Who's making us live under a strain?

CLINTON (*testily*) Circumstances—circumstances.

DELIA. Who's made the circumstances?

(*The front door is heard to slam.*
HARDACRE *enters hurriedly* L)

HARDACRE (*moving to* L *of Clinton*) You must be Mr Clinton. I'm Hardacre—spoke to you on the phone. Glad you took action at once. It's the only way. Take action. Get on with it, I always say. I nearly took it up with your Head Office.

CLINTON. I'm glad you didn't. I . . .

HARDACRE (*cutting in: roughly*) You understand how I'm fixed. This big loan for my Extension. I was doing it through Kettle. As a favour. We'd always got on nicely. Till today. (*He sits in the easy chair* LC) I say—*till today*.

STREET. Now, Alderman Hardacre, Mr Clinton knows all . . .

ACT III   MR KETTLE AND MRS MOON

HARDACRE (*cutting in; roughly*) A complete understanding—never a wrong word—*till today*.
MOON. You're repeating yourself, old man.
HARDACRE (*indignantly*) And I well might repeat myself; so would you if you were me. Do you know how much money's at stake with this Extension?
MOON (*keenly interested*) No. I've been wondering. Tell me.
HARDACRE (*indignantly*) I'm not going to tell you, Moon. And I'm surprised at you asking. It's my business, not yours.
MOON. You asked if I knew. No need to be so touchy.
HARDACRE (*angrily*) Touchy? Who says I'm touchy? And what I'm talking to you for, I don't know, Moon. What you're doing here, I can't imagine. No place for you. And no place for her, neither. If she were my wife . . .
DELIA (*cutting in*) I can think of fifty replies to that—all very rude. Now stop shouting.
HARDACRE (*loudly and angrily*) I'm not shouting. And anyhow, I haven't to take orders from you.

(*The* DOCTOR *enters from the bedroom*)

DOCTOR (*with authority*) Just a moment, please.
HARDACRE. And who are you?
DOCTOR (*with dignity*) I happen to be the doctor in charge of this case. And I'd be very glad if you wouldn't raise your voice so much. It's disturbing the patient. (*To Delia*) Are you Mrs Moon, by any chance?
DELIA. Yes. Why?
DOCTOR. The patient is asking if you are here.

(DELIA *moves towards the Doctor*)

No—no—you'll see him shortly. (*To Clinton*) Quite successful, I think, Mr Clinton.

(*The* DOCTOR *exits to the bedroom*)

HARDACRE (*in quiet but impressive tones*) All right, I'll talk quietly. But just listen to what I have to say. (*He is chiefly addressing Clinton*) If I don't see Kettle in the next half-hour—and get some attention from him—and an apology—the fat'll be in the fire. Because I've made an appointment to meet the editor of the *Brickmill Herald*—who's a very good friend of mine—at the Union Club in an hour's time. And unless I feel properly satisfied by that time—doctor or no doctor—I'll tell him all I know. And he'll print it.
CLINTON (*disturbed*) Alderman Hardacre—I assure you . . .
HARDACRE. Don't bother assuring me. Just show me Kettle in his right mind, that's all. And don't take too long about it—or else . . .
STREET. That's a bit hard, isn't it?

HARDACRE. You keep out of this.
STREET. Now—now—now!
HARDACRE (*rising*) Don't "now—now—now" me. Who d'you think I am—a lorry driver on the wrong side of the road?
STREET (*annoyed*) And who do you think I am—a constable on traffic duty?
MOON. Hardacre, old man, we know you've had a bad day . . .
HARDACRE. I don't think you've had a very good one, neither.
MOON. Nothing wrong with *my* day.
HARDACRE (*nastily*) That's what *you* think.
MOON (*annoyed*) Well, I ought to know, oughtn't I? I'm not going to ask *you* what kind of day I've had, am I?
HARDACRE. Perhaps it's as well.
MOON. What are you talking about?
DELIA (*quietly but impressively*) He's talking about me, Henry.
HARDACRE (*sitting in the easy chair*) Well, I'm not leaving you out.
DELIA. Not even out of the *Brickmill Herald*, probably. Unless George Kettle does a little grovelling, we all go into the *Herald*, do we? Well, I'm going to tell you something that will surprise you. It serves me right. I ought to have known better.
STREET. You mean this morning?
DELIA (*with spirit*) No, this afternoon. When I must have forgotten what a *man*—might have to put up with here. (*With a step towards Hardacre*) But though it'll serve me right, that doesn't excuse you. And now I'll tell *you* something—and you can publish this in the *Herald*, too. There are about a dozen of you here—all stinkers—and you're the chief reason why nobody in their senses ever wants to stay here. It isn't the factories and the smoke and the fog and the dirt and the dingy streets and the dreary little shops and the rissoles in the *Old Oak Café* and the Brown Windsor soup in the *County Hotel*—it's you—you.
HARDACRE (*angrily*) That'll do. We've heard enough from you.
MOON (*loudly*) Possibly, Hardacre, old man. But all the same . . .
HARDACRE (*cutting in; roughly*) Don't you start, Moon. When you can't even stop her wearing the trousers.
MOON (*indignantly*) Trousers? Who's talking about trousers?

(*The* DOCTOR *enters suddenly from the bedroom*)

DOCTOR (*moving behind the sofa*) Gentlemen, please. I should like your attention—before Mr Kettle joins us. He's dressing—and will be with us in a minute. I need your co-operation. This morning, a secondary self, hitherto suppressed, asserted itself. With the result that you found Mr Kettle saying things and doing things that seemed to you quite strange.
HARDACRE (*grimly*) I'll say he did. I thought he was drunk.

ACT III MR KETTLE AND MRS MOON 53

DOCTOR. A pardonable mistake, my dear sir. Alcohol helps to remove many of our social inhibitions.
HARDACRE (*fiercely*) I never touch it. Never a drop passes my lips . . .
DELIA (*cutting in; coldly*) Nobody's interested in your lips. Go on, Doctor.
DOCTOR (*very portentously*) I've been able to treat him successfully, restoring the primary self. He is—you may say—cured. But at this very early stage, please accept him exactly as he was before this unfortunate lapse.
HARDACRE. 'Ere, what do you . . .?
DOCTOR. No reproaches, please. If you co-operate with me, then your presence here will do more good than harm. It subjects him to a useful test. Most successful, I think we may say, Mr Clinton.
CLINTON. Very gratifying, Doctor.
DOCTOR. Thank you. A most promising method of treatment. And one that . . .
DELIA (*cutting in*) Just a minute.
DOCTOR (*moving to* R *of Delia; annoyed at being interrupted*) Well—I don't know what your interest is here, madam . . .
DELIA. Strictly personal—not scientific. What was this treatment?
DOCTOR. Well—if you must know, madam—shock followed almost immediately by a light hypnosis.
DELIA. He's knocked out—then just when he's coming round—you get to work on him—without asking his permission.
DOCTOR. In the circumstances—naturally I couldn't ask his permission. For his own good. I had to help him to suppress the secondary self and to restore the primary.
DELIA. How do you know which is the real George Kettle?
DOCTOR. That's beside the point. The primary self is successfully adjusted to life, the secondary self isn't. It's maladjusted, anti-social, childish, irresponsible, fanciful, incapable of playing a proper part in the modern social order. So the decision to restore the primary self is inevitable.
MOON. Absolutely. Very interesting, Doctor. Makes a chap think, doesn't it?
DELIA (*grimly*) It's making this chap think—very hard.
DOCTOR. Mrs—er—Moon, I've permitted you to stay because for some reason or other the patient particularly enquired if you were here. But I must ask for your co-operation, too—for *his* sake.
DELIA (*grimly*) Don't worry. He'll get it.
DOCTOR (*listening*) Sh! He's here.

(KETTLE *enters slowly from the bedroom. He is dressed in his bank manager's clothes and looks rather pale. His manner is meek and rather servile, in the sharpest contrast to his manner before now. He smiles sheepishly and apologetically to the company.* DELIA *regards him with horror; the men regard him approvingly*)

(*In the usual hearty style*) Well—Mr Kettle—feeling all right now, eh? Very different from what you did when you first came round—um?

KETTLE (*humbly*) Doctor, when I remember, I can't think what had taken possession of me. It was awful. I could hear myself saying the most shocking things. "There's that cunning old busybody, Superintendent Street," I was saying. "That stuffed shirt, Clinton, from the district Head Office. That idiot, Henry Moon," I was saying. "That bad-tempered miserable old skinflint, Hardacre."

HARDACRE (*angrily*) Here—what d'you mean . . .?

DOCTOR (*cutting in; with authority*) No, no, no, please. It may be necessary for him to explain . . .

DELIA (*cutting in*) Then it's my turn. What were you saying to yourself about me?

KETTLE (*crossing to* R *of Delia; alarmed and apologetic*) Oh—Mrs Moon—please don't ask me. I didn't really know what I was saying—thinking . . .

DELIA (*commandingly*) Go on. What about me?

KETTLE. It doesn't make sense. I was saying to myself, "That lovely enchanting creature, Delia Moon—what a pity she's such a coward."

DELIA (*moving to Kettle and staring hard at him; suspiciously*) George Kettle!

KETTLE (*with a sickly smile*) You see, Mrs Moon, I didn't know what I was saying. I told you it didn't make sense. (*He crosses to* R *of Clinton*) Excuse me, Mrs Moon. Oh—Mr Clinton.

CLINTON (*shaking hands with Kettle*) Nice to see you again, Mr Kettle. I came here for the afternoon—and couldn't leave without saying "Hello".

KETTLE (*humbly*) It's very good of you, Mr Clinton. I do appreciate it. I'm sorry I wasn't at the bank when you called—but I had some sort of accident.

CLINTON (*heartily*) Don't mention it, Kettle. These things will happen. All right now, I think?

KETTLE. Yes, thank you, Mr Clinton. But we don't often see you at our Brickmill branch—and I was hoping to talk things over.

CLINTON (*heartily*) We'll have that talk, next time. Here's Alderman Hardacre—wants to have a word with you.

(HARDACRE *rises*)

KETTLE (*crossing to* R *of Hardacre; apologetically*) Oh—Alderman Hardacre—you must be worrying about that Extension Loan, aren't you?

HARDACRE (*grimly*) Of course I am, Kettle. Spent all day worrying about it.

DOCTOR (*quickly*) Careful now.

KETTLE (*timidly eager*) I meant to tell you this morning I had a message from Head Office—it comes before the Board on Wednesday.

HARDACRE (*in a bullying tone*) You've put it to 'em properly, Kettle—hot and strong, eh?

KETTLE (*eagerly*) I can assure you I have, Alderman Hardacre—and I'm sorry you've been put to so much trouble.

HARDACRE (*moving to the door* L; *roughly*) Well, just be careful in future, Kettle.

KETTLE (*moving up* R *of the easy chair; humbly*) You can depend on me, Alderman Hardacre.

DELIA (*unable to restrain herself; disgusted*) Oh—my God!

KETTLE (*turning to face Delia; rather reproachfully*) Mrs Moon!

DELIA. Well, Mr Kettle?

KETTLE (*apologetically*) I suppose you're worried about the Infirmary Wireless Fund account?

DELIA. No, I'm not.

KETTLE. Oh!

DELIA. I'm worried about *you*.

KETTLE. I'm sorry. But really—I don't think it'll happen again.

DELIA. Don't bother about me. There must be somebody else you can apologize to. (*She moves abruptly to the desk*)

HARDACRE. Well, I'm off. Glad you've come to your senses, Kettle.

(DELIA *unobtrusively extracts the revolver from the desk drawer*)

KETTLE (*moving towards Hardacre*) Thank you, Alderman Hardacre.

(HARDACRE *exits abruptly* L *before Kettle can open the door for him*)

(*He turns to Street*) Superintendent, I'm very glad you're here. You'll remember I wrote to you about the parking regulations at our bank corner?

STREET. Came to see you about it this morning, Mr Kettle.

KETTLE. Oh—I hope I haven't inconvenienced you at all, Superintendent?

STREET. No, not much. But I don't know if the doctor wants us to talk about it now.

DOCTOR. Frankly, I'd rather you didn't.

KETTLE. Thank you, Doctor. I appreciate that, and I don't feel quite . . . (*He looks faint*)

(CLINTON *moves to the easy chair* LC, *turns it slightly, and* KETTLE *sits*)

CLINTON. Quite right. Don't rush things, Kettle, though I know how keen you are. But Dr Grenock's speaking for the bank, too—he's another member of the family.

KETTLE (*humbly*) I'm glad to hear it. And I'd like to say this before you go, Mr Clinton. The London and North Midland isn't just something that pays me money. I like to feel it's my friend.

CLINTON. It is, Kettle, it is.

KETTLE (*smiling apologetically*) I don't want to sound far-fetched. But in a way—because I owe it so much—I feel it's like a father and mother.

DELIA (*savagely*) Why don't you go and kiss it?

(KETTLE *leans back and looks half asleep*)

DOCTOR. Please! Well, gentlemen, you probably want to be off—and I must spend a few minutes giving my patient some advice about diet, sleep, that sort of thing. (*He glances at Kettle*)

CLINTON (*heartily*) Of course. Wonderful job, Dr Grenock. (*He glances at Kettle and lowers his voice*) He's all right, I suppose?

DOCTOR (*motioning them to the door* L) Yes—yes—a natural reaction.

(CLINTON *and* STREET *move to the door* L. MOON *rises and crosses above the sofa to Delia*)

CLINTON (*heartily*) Well, good night, Kettle.

DOCTOR (*crossing to Clinton and Street*) Bound to be rather exhausted—quite a natural reaction—but nothing to worry about.

(STREET, CLINTON *and the* DOCTOR *exit* L)

MOON. Better go home now, hadn't you, Delia?

DELIA (*moving to the sofa and sitting; rather grimly*) Not yet, Henry. But *you* go.

MOON (*moving* C) Well, as a matter of fact, I must do some work at the office—on this Murchison factory deal. They're waiting for me.

DELIA. Who's they? Miss Carson?

MOON (*with dignity*) As my assistant, Miss Carson will be there—of course.

DELIA. Off you go then, Henry.

(*The* DOCTOR *enters* L)

Don't keep Miss Carson waiting.

MOON. Good night, Kettle.

KETTLE (*sleepily*) Good night, Moon.

MOON (*crossing to the door* L; *to the Doctor*) First-class, Doctor—absolutely first-class. Wouldn't have missed it for anything. Wonderful what you fellows can do nowadays.

DOCTOR. Thank you, Mr Moon. Well—good night.

MOON. Good night.

(MOON *exits* L)

DOCTOR (*surprised that Delia does not depart*) Mrs Moon—aren't you going with your husband?
DELIA. No, he's going to be busy at the office.
DOCTOR. Yes—but . . .
DELIA. So I'm staying here.
DOCTOR. I don't think you ought.
DELIA. I do. But just—carry on.

(*The* DOCTOR, *after giving Delia a reproachful stare, moves to* R *of the easy chair and turns to Kettle*)

DOCTOR. Now, Mr Kettle, I don't want to tire you—and I shan't be long—but please pay attention.
KETTLE (*opening his eyes*) Yes, Doctor?
DOCTOR. That's it. Just keep looking at me. (*He turns and stares reproachfully at Delia*) Now what we must guard against is a sudden relapse. You wouldn't like that, would you?
KETTLE. No, I shouldn't.
DOCTOR. So I want you to follow my instructions very carefully. Now—lead your ordinary life, but avoid all excitement.
KETTLE. If I lead my ordinary life, there won't be any excitement.
DOCTOR (*ignoring this*) Eat plain wholesome food. No alcohol. No late hours. Avoid all over-stimulating experiences—perhaps you ought to buy a television set. As you're not married, we can ignore sex.
DELIA. Let's pretend it doesn't exist and we're all neuters.
DOCTOR (*crossing to Delia and standing over her; angrily*) Mrs Moon, I must ask you either to go or to keep quiet. Don't you realize that any interference at this stage in a hypnotic treatment can be extremely dangerous.
DELIA (*rising and backing a step or two away from the Doctor*) Yes, and this can be even more dangerous. (*She points the revolver at him*)
DOCTOR (*alarmed*) How dare you! Put down that revolver at once.
DELIA (*sharply*) Sit down.

(*The* DOCTOR *sits reluctantly on the sofa*)

(*She moves behind the sofa and threatens the Doctor with the revolver*) Let me explain, first, that I'm not a bad shot. I shan't kill you, of course—but I'll aim at your kneecap and put you out for months. That is, *if* you don't do what I say.
DOCTOR. This is preposterous. Why should I do what you say? What's the meaning of all this?

DELIA. Haven't they ever told you anything about women, Doctor Thing? Y'know, on the whole, even now, we're very docile passive creatures, easily imposed upon by you men, ready to believe all your nonsense and obey your idiotic rules. But one thing can make us desperate, rebellious, prepared to risk anything. Love, Doctor.

DOCTOR (*uneasily*) I'm quite aware that at times the sexual impulse . . .

DELIA (*cutting in; ruthlessly*) Shut up!

DOCTOR (*rising; indignantly*) If you think, madam . . .

DELIA (*turning the revolver on him; fiercely*) And *sit down*.

(*The* DOCTOR *sits reluctantly on the sofa*)

I'd almost enjoy shooting you—you miserable little man. For years, I've waited to love—and be loved. And today it happened —we found each other. We were wonderfully happy together. But then I did a stupid, cowardly thing. He asked me to run away with him—and I refused. But when I came back, ready to go away with him, I found *you* here—turning him into a sanctimonious snivelling dummy again. He'd stopped being like that. He'd come alive. Then, you got hold of him when he was only half conscious and mesmerized him into misery again. He was awake—and you wanted him sleep-walking again, like the rest of you.

DOCTOR (*rising; desperately*) Mrs Moon—I assure you—I was only . . .

DELIA (*fiercely*) Undo what you've done—or I'll pull this trigger—I swear I will.

DOCTOR (*desperately*) Kettle—I appeal to you—as a decent law-abiding citizen . . .

KETTLE (*quietly*) No, Doctor. It's between you two.

DELIA (*fiercely*) Go on. Do whatever you ought to do to free him completely.

DOCTOR (*crossing to* C; *resigning himself*) Very well. But first you must realize what you're wanting me to do. What you will have is an anti-social, childish, irresponsible type, incapable of playing a proper part in the modern social order.

DELIA (*enthusiastically*) I know.

DOCTOR (*severely*) An obvious misfit, rebellious, extravagant, liable to over-indulgence in alcohol—sex . . .

DELIA (*delighted*) I know—I know.

DOCTOR (*very severely*) And you'll probably be as bad as he is.

DELIA (*delighted*) I do hope so.

DOCTOR (*glaring at her; furiously*) Strumpet!

DELIA (*wildly*) And the strumpet shall sound. (*She points the revolver at him*) This is your last chance—one—two . . .

DOCTOR (*in a panic*) Stop, stop. I'll try. (*He turns to Kettle*) Now—Kettle—look at me—please.

ACT III   MR KETTLE AND MRS MOON

KETTLE (*rising; coolly*) No, Doctor. I'm tired of looking at you.

(*The exterior lights brighten as the clouds clear and the rain ceases*)

DELIA (*astonished*) George!

(KETTLE *crosses to* DELIA *and they embrace*)

KETTLE. Well, Delia darling, you've seen what it would be like if I stayed here—*now* when do we go?

DELIA (*delighted*) Tonight. Now. But I'd made up my mind before. I rang up to tell you.

KETTLE. I didn't know. So I felt I had to make you understand.

DOCTOR (*tapping Kettle on the arm; astonished*) But what about the treatment I gave you?

KETTLE. My dear chap, you couldn't hypnotize a rabbit. (*He takes the revolver from Delia*) By the way, the revolver isn't loaded. (*He tosses the revolver into the easy chair*) So don't go and make a fuss about it.

DOCTOR. I won't. So long as you won't say anything to Mr Clinton.

KETTLE. Clinton! I don't propose to set eyes on him again. Why?

DOCTOR (*confidentially*) Between ourselves—I've only just qualified as a psychiatrist. I'm an ear, nose, and throat man really.

KETTLE. How are *my* ears, nose, and throat?

DOCTOR (*seriously*) I had a good look round. All in excellent condition.

KETTLE (*leading the Doctor to the door* L) Thank you, Doctor. And I don't think we need keep you—good-bye.

DOCTOR. Good day to you.

DELIA (*calling*) Good-bye.

(*The* DOCTOR *exits* L)

We'll go off in my car, I packed two bags—they're in the car—and I could start packing for you while you change your clothes.

KETTLE (*surprised*) Clothes? (*He looks with disgust at his clothes*) Oh—of course—I'm wearing these dam' things. (*He tears his collar clean off, then hurriedly removes his coat*)

(DELIA *exits to the bedroom.* KETTLE *crosses to the radiogram and switches on the record.*

MRS TWIGG *enters from the kitchen. She wears her outdoor clothes and is carrying a blancmange*)

MRS TWIGG (*shouting over the music*) Mr Kettle—I've made you a shape.

KETTLE. All right. But you'll have to eat it yourself. We're going. I'll write to you. And remember me to Monica.

(MONICA *enters* L. *She is wearing outdoor clothes*)

MONICA. You can remember yourself to Monica. Did I hear you say you were going?
KETTLE. Yes. As soon as we've packed a few things.

(DELIA *enters from the bedroom. She carries a suitcase, Kettle's easy clothes, and a bundle of other clothing for packing*)

DELIA (*as she enters*) Here you are, darling. (*She sees Mrs Twigg and Monica*) Oh! (*She hands the easy clothes to Kettle, then puts the case on the floor* C, *kneels and commences packing*)

MONICA. If you two are going, so am I. And you can give me a lift.

KETTLE. Now, wait a minute, Monica . . .

MONICA. Oh—don't worry—I know she's got you. I won't have another try. But if that Superintendent's gone away—all baffled—he'll try an' take it out of me next.

MRS TWIGG. I'm afraid she's right—an' I wish you could give her a lift—'cos I don't trust them lorry drivers an inch.

KETTLE. All right, Mrs Twigg.

(KETTLE *exits to the bedroom.* MONICA *kneels* R *of the case and helps* DELIA *to pack*)

MONICA (*scornfully*) Catch me askin' one of them. Mrs Moon, how about me bein' a personal maid for a week or two?

DELIA. No, I couldn't live up to your performance, Monica. But we can drop you at my sister's—for a night or two—she lives just the other side of Birmingham.

MONICA (*suspiciously*) Has she a lot of children—an' no help?

DELIA. Her husband's a television producer.

MONICA (*ecstatically*) Hurry up—let's get going.

(*The radiogram comes into a loud passage.*
KETTLE *enters from the bedroom. He carries some clothes for packing, which he hands to Delia. He has changed into his easy clothes.* MRS TWIGG *stares at them with her mouth open for a moment*)

MRS TWIGG (*shouting*) Well—there's one thing—it's stopped raining. I say—it's stopped raining.

The CURTAIN *quickly falls*

FURNITURE AND PROPERTY LIST

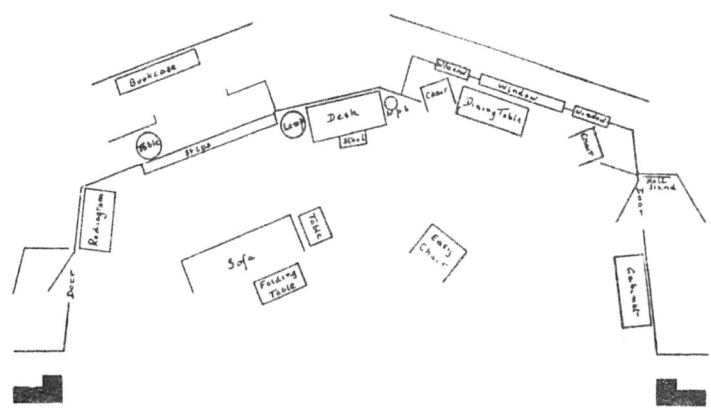

ACT I

On stage—Sofa. *On it:* cushions, ashtray and copy of *Birmingham Post* on left arm
           Folding table. *On it:* tray, tray-cloth, toast-rack, 2 pieces of toast, butter dish, marmalade, teapot, milk jug, sugar basin, packet of cornflakes, tea and cereal plates, cup and saucer, knife, fork, spoon, tea spoon, copy of *The Times*
           Easy chair. *On it:* cushion
           Table (L of sofa). *On it:* box with cigarettes, matches, ashtray
           Cabinet (down L). *On it:* silver tray, bottle of whisky, 2 whisky glasses, sherry glass, syphon of soda, ashtray
                In cupboard: decanter of sherry
           Dining-table. *On it:* plant in pot
           2 dining-chairs
           Desk. *On it:* vase of flowers, telephone, telephone directory-pad, message pad, pencil
           Waste-paper basket
           Stool
           Standard lamp
           Coal scuttle (down R of sofa)
           On floor below sofa: KETTLE's easy shoes
           Radiogram. *On turntable:* record Borodin's *Polovtsian Dances from Prince Igor*
           Carpet on floor
           Rugs
           Window curtains
           Pictures on walls
           Electric-candle wall-brackets R and L
           Light switch below door L
           In hall: hall-stand
Door L closed
Door R closed

MR KETTLE AND MRS MOON 63

Window open at bottom
Curtains open
Light fittings off
Off stage—Duster (MRS TWIGG)
        Shooting game (tied with string) (KETTLE)
        Bowler hat (KETTLE)
        Drumstick (KETTLE)
        Pair of cymbals (KETTLE)
        Jacket with pipe, matches and pouch of tobacco in pocket (KETTLE)
        Basket. *In it:* food parcels (DELIA)
        Dress box (DELIA)
Personal—DELIA: spectacles

ACT II

Strike—Dirty whisky glass
      Dirty sherry glass
      Shooting game and darts
      Plant from dining-table
      Drumstick
      Basket of parcels
      Cymbals
Set—Dining-table a little down stage
    On dining-table: table mats, salad bowl with remains of salad, salad servers, dish with pineapple, cruet
    In table drawer: revolver
    Transfer decanter of sherry to dining-table
    Set chair R of dining-table to above it
    Transfer ashtray from easy chair to left arm of sofa
    On sofa at left end: Delia's handbag
    Move coal scuttle down R of sofa
    On cabinet R: 2 whisky glasses
    On desk: 2 dinner plates with remains of meal and knives and forks
    Folding table-tray (below left end of sofa). *On it:* tray, ashtray, 2 tablespoons, coffee cup and saucer
    On floor below sofa: empty Hock bottle
    On table L *of sofa:* coffee-pot, cheese carton on plate, shrimp carton on plate, side plate, 2 small knives, 2 Hock glasses, napkin
    On sofa: Delia's housecoat draped over back, napkin on left arm
    On floor below right end of sofa: coffee cup and saucer on side plate

Telephone receiver off
Hall door closed
Kitchen door closed
Window closed
Window curtains closed
Wall-brackets on
Standard lamp on
Personal—KETTLE: pipe
        MOON: umbrella, watch

ACT III

Door L closed
Door R closed
Window closed
Window curtains open
Lights on
Off stage—Blancmange (MRS TWIGG)
        Suitcase, clothing (DELIA)
        Clothing (KETTLE)

LIGHTING PLOT

PROPERTY FITTINGS REQUIRED—standard lamp, 2 pairs electric-candle wall-brackets (practical), floods outside window, flood outside arch up R, strips outside doors R and L

INTERIOR. A living-room. The same scene throughout

THE MAIN ACTING AREAS ARE—at a sofa RC, at an easy chair LC, up RC, C and up LC

THE APPARENT SOURCES OF LIGHT ARE—in daytime—a window up L, and at night—a standard lamp up C and wall-brackets R and L

ACT I   Morning

To open: Effect of a dull, rainy morning
　　　　　Onstage lighting, dim
　　　　　Strips outside doors R and L, on
　　　　　Floods outside window and arch, on
　　　　　Brackets, off
　　　　　Standard lamp, off

Cue 1　MRS TWIGG switches on wall-brackets　　　　　(page 2)
　　　Snap in wall-brackets
　　　Bring up onstage lighting

Cue 2　KETTLE switches on standard lamp　　　　　(page 18)
　　　Snap in standard lamp
　　　Bring up lights to cover

Cue 3　KETTLE switches off wall-brackets　　　　　(page 19)
　　　Snap out wall-brackets
　　　Reduce general lighting

ACT II   Afternoon

To open: Dull daylight outside window
　　　　　Onstage lights, full up
　　　　　Strips outside doors R and L, on
　　　　　Floods outside window and arch, on
　　　　　Brackets, on
　　　　　Standard lamp, on

No cues

ACT III   Early evening

To open: Lights as at the end of the previous Act

Cue 4　KETTLE: "... looking at you."　　　　　(page 59)
　　　Bring up exterior lighting

www.ingramcontent.com/pod-product-compliance
Ingram Content Group UK Ltd.
Pitfield, Milton Keynes, MK11 3LW, UK
UKHW021847210426
5322IPUK00022B/512